T0169929

RAYMOND WILLIAMS

FROM WALES TO THE WORLD

RAYMOND WILLIAMS

FROM WALES TO THE WORLD

EDITED BY
STEPHEN
WOODHAMS

MODERN
WALES

PARTHIAN

Parthian, Cardigan SA43 1ED
www.parthianbooks.com
First published in 2021
© 2021 The Contributors
All Rights Reserved
ISBN 978-1-913640-92-7
eISBN 978-1-913640-93-4
Cover design by www.theundercard.co.uk
Typeset by Syncopated Pandemonium
Printed and bound by xxx
Published with the financial support of the Welsh Books
Council.
The Modern Wales series receives support from the Rhys
Davies Trust

the RHYS DAVIES TRUST

British Library Cataloguing in Publication Data
A cataloguing record for this book is available from the
British Library.

Contents

Commendations   vii

Acknowledgements   xi

Wales and Beyond
Stephen Woodhams   1

A Longer History
Stephen Woodhams   15

Crossing the Border
Elizabeth Allen   49

'A culture where I can breathe'
Stephen Woodhams   79

Dream of a Country
Elizabeth Allen   105

The Purposes of Adult Education
Derek Tatton   135

Welsh European
Hywel Dix   157

Sowing the Seeds of Change
Hywel Dix   185

Resources for a journey of hope
Stephen Woodhams   215

Contributor Biographies   263

My father always considered himself a Welsh European, and these essays offer an illuminating study of this aspect of his identity.

Merryn Williams

Commendations

Steve Woodhams, author of *History in the Making*, a fabulous pioneering study of Raymond Williams, E. P. Thompson and the British New Left, brings another excellent contribution to the field, this time taking Williams as sole protagonist. *Raymond Williams: From Wales to the World* offers significant insights into Williams as a 'Welsh European', who taking his ground in the border country, engaged the world beyond. This book deserves to be widely read; affirming the life and work of Raymond Williams continues to those of us who care for democracy, common culture and communalistic values.

Yasuo Kawabata, Chair of Raymond Williams
Kenkyukai (Society), Tokyo

Raymond Williams, who was my teacher at Cambridge, was an extraordinarily perceptive critic of culture. He was deeply rooted in Welsh culture and tradition; but as Stephen Woodhams has so ably demonstrated, Williams' ideas, concepts, methods of analysis have a bearing on cultural hermeneutics in other parts of the world. Woodhams has established cogently the global relevance of Raymond Williams. This is a first-rate book that situates Williams in a newer context of understanding.

Wimal Dissanayake, *Raymond Williams through Sri Lankan eyes*, Hawaii and Sri Lanka

Crossing borders real and imaginative, this work acknowledges Raymond Williams to be a significant European thinker in contemporary society.

Monika Seidl, *About Raymond Williams*, Vienna

Raymond Williams: From Wales to the World is a valuable contribution to studies of Raymond Williams, especially situating his work in relation to the social history of Wales. The book identifies Williams' differences from other contemporary theorists such as Louis Althusser, and his dialogue with the ecological writings of Rudolf Bahro, with whom Williams shared a commitment to fundamental democracy. The guide to sources, including audio-visual material, will be invaluable for readers of Williams' extensive work. The book makes a convincing case for Raymond Williams as a Welsh European.

Alan O'Connor, *Raymond Williams*, Toronto

Wales, situated immediately to the west of England and Bengal situated ten thousand kilometres east of England are both border countries. In engagement with one of Williams' contemporaries, I have felt a politico-spiritual camaraderie between Wales and Bengal, in among other things, our love-hate relationship with England. The life and work of Raymond Williams connects us, minds that live and die in the creative tension of margins. I can only congratulate Steve for giving us impetus to recognise the relevance of Williams for those of us outside European borders.

Sunandan Roy Chowdhury, Sampark publishing house, Kolkata

Raymond Williams belonged to that most original generation of interwar intellectuals and activists yet knew where he came from and what he 'came to say'. *Raymond Williams: From Wales to the World* makes these origins and their effects clear. More than that, it convincingly demonstrates that however rooted to a particular place and people, Williams was also a cosmopolitan world figure. He spoke to us all, with what is now recognisable as a Welsh accent, and deserves to be read everywhere.

Michael Merrill, New York

Acknowledgements

This book has been in the making far longer than decency should permit, and I would like to thank all involved for their forbearance. I have certainly learnt much, working with people from varied backgrounds; the contrasts between their chapters has been both informative and enjoyable. A warm thank you to Merryn Williams for support over the book's long gestation; the recent revival of Raymond Williams' work owes much to her labours. Related to Merryn, genial thanks go to the home of the Raymond Williams Papers in Swansea, and especially Katrina Legg the Archivist, who assisted in numerous enquiries. Acknowledgement is extended to the Raymond Williams Foundation and Raymond Williams Society for support over the years. Many people have given intellectual stimulus, and appreciation is offered to Michael Rustin, the late Paul Hirst, Dai Smith, Daniel Williams and Yasuo Kawabata. During the writing of this book, lights have gone out in the world, and the passing of Eric Hobsbawm and Stuart Hall are losses we share in common.

A warm thank you to Bob Foster for his encouragement and for producing the graph on page 15 based on an original that appeared in Gwyn Williams' *When Was Wales?*

Warmest wishes to Shivdeep Grewal for keeping the mind exercised. To Parmod Khokhar, Margarida Sousa, the two beings named Tiny and others on more than two legs for the best years of life. Amid painful experiences, this book has been a sanctuary sustained by special people. Their names are not given here, but they know who they are – thank you for being there.

A sincere thank you to every one associated with Parthian Books for the excellent efficiency and good nature that has made this book possible.

This book together with others appears in the centenary of the birth of Raymond Williams and gratitude must be paid to all those who are working to make the occasion of lasting value by placing Williams as a figure not only of historical significance but one who speaks to our times and the future.

Stephen Woodhams

1

Wales and Beyond

Stephen Woodhams

Raymond Williams has never been a figure easy to place. His self-description as 'Writer' encapsulates much of the reputation yet leaves sufficient open to be explained. A consequence has been closer attempted designations, of which perhaps best known is 'Cambridge literary critic'. Though commonly used, this however limits Williams by place, tradition and intellectual scope and fails to comprehend the breadth of his engagement. The acclamation, 'founder of cultural studies', is not unrelated to literary critic, but captures the idea that Williams moved on, as it were, from *Culture and Society* to *The Long Revolution*, engaging with continental European thinking where, from the early twentieth century, the study of culture was understood and accepted as a science. Other titular headings have followed; 'European intellectual' overtly places Williams in a series of twentieth-century figures and has the advantage of situating him among his contemporaries on a broader more appropriate scale. Each of the headings helped fill out the envelope, adding substance, yet we need still the generic term of writer if the full body of work and its creator is to be kept as a single whole.

To approach Williams in academic terms would, given the compartmentalisation of knowledge imposed by the academy, mean missing the greater part of his work. The creative writer for fiction and documentary does not sit easily with the history of reading or education, any more than a regular television column does with the abstract theoretician of culture and determinism. The division so regularly imposed on Williams, as between critic and novelist, has served to obscure the integral singleness of the writing. This failure of understanding was once commonly found, even among those who might be expected to know better; for *Politics and Letters*, the interviews on the novels were conducted in 1978, a full year after those done for the rest of the book where most attention was on the critical works. Yet, rather than taking the opportunity of this separate questioning to delve in depth, there is a bias toward overt politics in the interviewer's questions, with a consequence that much else, such as the emotions of characters which in places make up the intricacies of a narrative, are left under-explored.

In similar manner, Williams' years in adult education have at times been left to discrete discussion. The ascriptions, whether Cambridge literary critic, or founder of cultural studies, require their subject to be of an academic stand-ing as measured by current criteria, where being anything other than inside the academy will simply not do. This is ahistorical of course, given that for a long period intellectual advances were more likely from outside the university classroom domain of upper middle-class Anglican males. One source of innovation arrived with refugee intellectuals from fascist-controlled continental Europe, who found work in the more liberal environs of university extra-mural or extension faculties. This is an as yet under-researched dimension of Williams' maturation, but one that may bear fruit. How far a work such as *The Long Revolution* can be said to benefit from the presence in the Oxford Delegacy of forced migrants from the imminent ravages of a war-torn continent is not an easily answerable question. This 1930s migration remains an as yet submerged background to the development of Williams' thinking.

The point brings us to what earlier was cited as a third alternative for identifying Williams, that of the European intellectual. One qualification to be inserted with this measure is that unlike, for instance, Eric Hobsbawm, we should not expect to find Williams presiding alongside other senior figures over their intellectual trade. Yet, of course, that is just the point. Eric Hobsbawm was a historian, and history as a subject could presume a hierarchy whereby its finest practitioners might meet, debate and even adjudicate. Raymond Williams did not work according to academic subject, but wrote across intellectual boundaries, pursuing his own path as an original intelligence. In this manner, Williams engaged with diverse thinkers across Europe, sometimes using Cambridge as a place where they might find a voice, or at other times himself venturing out, as he says, to the cities he had seen and in which he found means to explore and exchange thinking.

The novels, his role in adult learning, and as a European intellectual are directly responded to here, while the conventional views of him as Cambridge literary critic or founder of cultural studies are displaced. The book locates movements out, along the different channels of Raymond's mind, from the vantage point of Wales, premising that it was the solidity of this beginning that enabled him to practice so many forms yet keep each together in a life that retained at its centre a memory of the Black Mountains. Television critic and historian, playwright and theoretician were made possible within a single figure because emotionally he had, early in life, internalised a secure base from which to offer and receive change within an active process of engagement. Raymond Williams was born in Pandy on the Welsh Border, five years before the General Strike of 1926. The coincidence of an event that had dramatic effects in South Wales, and over Raymond's formative years, was to result in a lasting influence on him; one confirmed by the strike's central place in his first published novel, *Border Country*. Yet Pandy was not in the Coalfield, the epicentre of the events of that year. Rather the village was settled in the lee of the Black Mountains. A subject in interviews and recurring in his novels, this physical landscapes' most emphatic presence was as the central character of his last and tragically unfinished work, *People of the Black Mountains*. Settling the life of the young Raymond, or Jim as he was known in his home village, was the circumstance of home. His mother worked first to maintain house for father and son, and then on the field and garden that the Williams' used to augment the wages of a railway signalman. This, his father's occupation, figures as a spine in *Border Country*, and appeared in films such as *The Country and The City*, while the man himself was, up until his death in 1958, an immense presence in the son's life.

The appearance in 2008 of Dai Smith's biography, *Raymond Williams: A Warrior's Tale*, made clear the means by which features from early years were kept as memory, and eventually adapted to use in his writing. The life and the work were a unity, so making for a depth of experience that gave the writing what has been described as layered meaning. In short – the words had substance. Raymond Williams went on to write of his experience and offer it to others at times in the form of short biographical accounts. The extraordinary variance in forms of writing, the published interviews and broadcasts have induced increasing responses across Europe and beyond. His was a departure from expectations – working class, Welsh, Cambridge English, adult-education tutor, and then Cambridge's first Professor of Drama. On the assumed terms of some, it did not add up. An added final identity was the return to the border, a cottage in the hills above Pandy, where he could write and of course see his beloved Black Mountains. He had become besieged; requests to speak here, write a few words there, the demands went on. The cottage at Craswall was perhaps a means of creating at least some distance, setting a boundary; enabling the necessary time and space to pursue the endless stream of writing that from early in life he set himself. His work addressed global experiences; in *Border Country*, the pull of return yet its impossibility, in *The Fight for Manod*, the need for the development of land yet the threatened loss of localised control. Williams recognised the connections, local to global and back to local in ways that became more commonplace only years later. That which Williams wrote and spoke about most immediate to his own native country, was, in 2003, collected and presented by Daniel Williams in *Who Speaks for Wales?* The first extract dates from 1971 and indicates the direction of Williams' thinking in relation to a country to which he had made a partial return. It is a short essay responding to Ned Thomas' *The Welsh Extremist*, and provides the book with its title.

> I used to think that born into a Border country, at once physical, economic and cultural, my own relationship to the problem of Wales was especially problematic. But I now see, from Ned Thomas, among others, that it was characteristic. I remember focusing first on the powerful political culture of industrial South Wales.
>
> But there was always another idea of Wales: the more enclosed, mainly rural, more Welsh-speaking west and north. For me, in the beginning, that was much more remote. It was a commonplace that in consciousness there is often a great distance between what can be called but are not really two halves of the country. In the last decade

especially, and to a large extent because of what had happened to the earlier and wider movements in politics and education, another idea of Wales, drawn from its alternative source, has come through in the campaigns of Plaid Cymru and the Welsh Language Society.

Ned Thomas has written a description of his own experience and position relating to modern Welsh literature and the feel of the language. But from that local and specific idea of Wales he comes to conclusions which I would wholly endorse: that the only thing to do is 'to live out the tension, to try to work it out by changing the situation'.

This means challenging personally and publicly and from wherever we are, the immense imperatives which are not only flattening but preventing the realities of identity and culture. It is a cause better than national and more than international, for in its varying forms it is a very general human and social movement.

Since 1989 the name Raymond Williams has continued to appear on the cover of books, whether collections of his writings, critical essays or biography. Recently the output has been substantially advanced with the republication of a number of his books. Raymond Williams came to refer to himself as a Welsh European; that he could carry each of these terms equally was in no small part because he lived both. He had crossed borders in person on numerous occasions since his youth, later coming to address audiences in many places while exchanging ideas in print and speech.

From an early date, whether on drama or, slightly later, culture, his writings reveal an intellectual internationalism that did not become familiar perhaps until the seventies. As he wrote, he distilled these influences to produce not an arcane vocabulary in the manner of some, but a mode where meaning was densely layered yet located in a recognisable landscape. 'Culture is Ordinary', one of his earliest and finest pieces, starts with a bus ride from Hereford into his native Black Mountains. He is leading us into his thesis yet refers to the landscape through which the bus is passing. Later in the essay, he highlights sharp differences and antagonism by way of description of a tearoom in Cambridge, and the manner of speech used to display arrogant self-assuredness. Toward the essay's end, three swans on a lake are seemingly casually referred to, each being used for casting a wish. Yet in between these deceptively simple references, is woven an argument that defies standard interpretation of 'culture' to claim a place for people and ways of life with which Raymond Williams is intimately familiar. His own anchoring is through the knowable community that goes to make the Black Mountains, the place, he said, that he could see in his mind irrespective of present residence or physical distance.

An ability to turn ideas into a form of writing which, though notoriously deep could yet refer to the familiar, was arguably a skill gained from direct experience. As an adult-education tutor, Williams encountered the difficulty of integrating personal contributions brought to a class with ideas from inside the academy. Before then had been the experience of an oral culture in which he had grown up, where learning was respected and where the moving out to other worlds was familiar. In Wales, children maturing to move out from their home into school teaching, the ministry, civil service and law was not something that earned rejection but carried respect and was even expected. A reference to this condition was made in a conversation with his contemporary Richard Hoggart and published in the first issue of *New Left Review* in 1960. Yet, from his fiction we learn how movement out also carried anxiety, as so poignantly recreated in *Border Country*. The return of Matthew to be met as Jim, and the tension this double being creates, is intensely present in a scene where for Matthew/Jim standing beyond a door, aware of a conversation in the room behind and how he is being situated in the words, raises an anger which yet he does not feel able to let break through.

> As the door closed behind him, he stood in the passage fighting down the anger. He had learned very thoroughly to be ashamed of anger, and certainly it could be blamed, here in this anxious house. Yet he could not much longer go on accepting the unacceptable terms in which he was received. But the thread of the anger was confused. If he worked it loose, he could not know where it would lead.

In another scene, Ellen, Jim/Matthew's mother, had spoken of the ordinariness of people visiting to seek news of Harry following his stroke and, too, that they should naturally speak of the son's presence now, when otherwise he was away elsewhere. Ellen recalled also how, even though Harry had needed his son, he had been hesitant to ask for him to leave his work and come home. If it is his mother's words that the reader is hearing, it is into Matthew's complex emotions that they are drawn:

> Matthew drew in his breath. As he looked away he heard the separate language in his mind, the words of his ordinary thinking. He was trained to detachment: the language itself consistently abstracting and generalising, supported him in this. And the detachment was real in another way. He felt in this house both a child and a stranger. He could not speak as either; could not speak really as himself at all, but only in the terms that this pattern offered. At the same time, and quite physically, the actual crisis took its course.

The biographical features of Raymond Williams' early life offer obvious connection with Wales. Later, however, these associations take on a different manner. In the interviews that make up *Politics and Letters*, there occurs an as yet little-researched comment that in the later fifties he began to reread the history of Wales. This would have been difficult to achieve, and how Williams carried out this re-education bears further investigation. From around 1968, however, an altogether different situation emerged. The part move to a cottage on the border meant that opportunities to talk with writers and thinkers in Wales became more available. The prospect in *The Fight for Manod*, of Matthew working at the new Institute and Library for Industrial Wales, is a theme that might reasonably have come to Williams out of the kinds of work going on in different forms and places and with which he was gaining contact. Written over two phases, the first between 1965 and 1969, the second 1974 to 1978, meant that *The Fight for Manod* had time to absorb diverse expressions of cultural politics. Organisational forms varied as between Cymdeithas yr Iaith Gymraeg from 1963, the 'new left' wing of a reinvigorated Plaid Cymru and Llafur: The Welsh Labour History Society from 1970, pulling together differing, and often opposing, constituencies of interests and skills. Writing and publishing initiatives, long a prime means for expressing a sense of Wales, continued to struggle to be started and survive; *Poetry Wales* (1965), *Planet: The Welsh Internationalist* (1970), *Arcade: Wales Fortnightly* (1980–1982), *Radical Wales* (1983–1992). Then, catching the popular need to be engaged, were ongoing protests at the flooding of valleys with water dammed for the benefit of the English midlands and Liverpool. The 'National Question' was indeed again on the move though not in the conventional political calculations weighed only in votes. It can only here be an observation, but Raymond Williams was himself a crossroads, through which moved ideas connecting people and places, while at the same time he independently fashioned his own often more penetrating analyses. It was this working on the border, moving out to the cities where he spoke and discussed; then back to those people working in his native land, that made Raymond Williams a Welsh European. The ideas were important, but it was through his own life, that the step beyond England was made possible, and which repositioned Cambridge as only one vantage point among networks that transcended such educational and cultural destinations whether in England or Wales.

* * * * *

There is a forward momentum in time underlying the present book. Dai Smith's authorised biography, *Raymond Williams: A Warrior's Tale*, provided a new and detailed insight, one that few else could have written and which had not previously been possible. Any reader is directed toward that work, where understanding of its subject starts from the position that in Raymond Williams, life and work were an integral whole. The present book is indebted to Dai Smith but necessarily must move beyond the year where *A Warrior's Tale* ends in order to address Raymond Williams as his own engagement with Wales became more open. The word 'open' is used deliberately because when *Border Country* was published, his very personal attachment to the country came as something of a surprise to some. This attachment, however, has been affirmed in the collection of Williams' writings and interviews, *Who Speaks for Wales?* It was the first time Williams' commentaries on Wales had been brought together and, with the fine essay that forms the first part, the achievement of Daniel Williams' efforts is, here, apparent throughout.

Raymond Williams: From Wales to the World has been written with the intent that it should be readily accessible, and the academic ritual of burdening texts with references has therefore been replaced with a short list at the end of each chapter citing the main works consulted. Accessibility is the intent, too, in indicating how Williams may be approached. It is hoped that in citing Raymond Williams not only in print but through audio-visual and online, readers will be able to appreciate the breadth and scope of one of the twentieth century's most substantial intellectuals, and our continuing need for him if the long revolution he set out for us is to be realised.

Raymond Williams

'Culture is Ordinary', 1958, reprinted in *The Raymond Williams Reader*, Blackwell, 2001.

Border Country, 1960, Library of Wales, Parthian, 2006.

The Long Revolution, 1961, Parthian, 2011.

Second Generation, 1964, Hogarth, 1988.

The Fight for Manod, 1979, Hogarth, 1988.

Politics and Letters, 1979, Verso, 2015.

People of the Black Mountains, 1: The Beginning, 1989, Paladin, 1990.

People of the Black Mountains, 2: The Eggs of the Eagle, 1990, Paladin, 1992.

Who Speaks for Wales? Raymond Williams, edited Daniel Williams, UWP, 2003.

Other works

Mike Dibb, *The Country and The City*, 1979.

Dai Smith, *Raymond Williams: A Warrior's Tale*, Parthian, 2008.

Colin Thomas, *Border Crossing*, BBC4 tx 26/01/05.

Stephen Woodhams, *History in the Making*, Merlin, 2001.

2

A Longer History

Stephen Woodhams

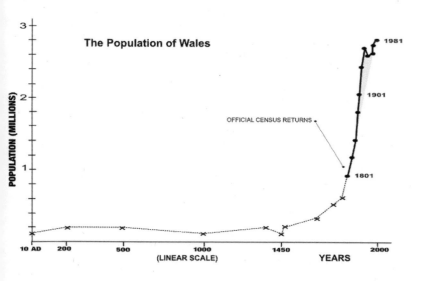

The Population of Wales

POPULATION (MILLIONS)

OFFICIAL CENSUS RETURNS

1981

1901

1801

10 AD   200   500   1000   1450   2000

(LINEAR SCALE)

YEARS

Look at this graph, a simplified outline of Welsh population growth. Is there a peak more jagged in Snowdonia?

That right angle in the late eighteenth century is the population explosion. Together with the conquest of energy and steam and the breakneck growth of industrial society, it created modern Britain, western Europe [and], in terms of the human race as a biological species occupying a particular stretch of territory in Europe and its offshore islands, that explosion turned everything that had gone before into a kind of prehistory.

Consider some literally vital statistics. There was something over half a million people in Wales in the middle of the eighteenth century when, in every area, numbers started to multiply. From the 1780s when iron strikes its roots in the east, the increase becomes cumulative. During the first half of the nineteenth century, it is breakneck. By 1921, there were 2,600,000 people in Wales. Over little more than four generations, the population has nearly quintupled. These changes seem to me to rank with the discovery of steam.

That explosion, so tellingly expressed by the historian Gwyn Alf Williams, is our base. In a few decades, the population had migrated internally so that a majority of the country's people soon existed in and by the extraction of coal and the production of metal in the south-east corner. The modern history of Wales, Glanmor Williams stressed, started from the 1760s, and that is the substance of the present chapter. What, it is stressed here, marks Wales and the Welsh, was a capacity to create a culture both in the sense of a way of life and as creative expression. The two modes entwined in hymn singing, band playing, acting, playing ball, or building temples that became chapels, miners institutes and libraries, proving the means through which further learning was sought.

The chapter seeks to sketch a history whereby the figure of Raymond Williams may be realised against a longer time frame than might be usual for a more intimate portrait. We set out chronologically a little before 'The Crucible' from whence emerged modern Wales, cross-analysing demography, industry and culture, to end at the formative moment of 1926. Beyond lay those turbulent years, of which a fine account has already been told by Dai Smith in his celebrated biography *A Warrior's Tale*, when Raymond Williams, matured and set off, first to school in Abergavenny, then on to Cambridge University and world war, and so with the Army to Normandy, Brussels and over the German border into a then crumbling Reich.

Suggestion that early modern Wales could be envisaged as conservative in its allegiances may surprise. Yet, before 1700 Wales not only conformed to the Established (Anglican) Church but had previously a long heritage of Catholicism that continued well beyond the Reformation. In the Civil War, while there had been supporters and soldiers for the beleaguered Parliament in London, the predominant tendency was for Wales to side with the King and indeed at one point in the War supplied, as did Ireland, a substantial military presence in the Royalist ranks. Given the outpouring of radical Dissent in England in these years, continuance of a Catholicism, practiced secretly and away from the gaze of the inspectors of the new religious order, might suggest that Wales was as far from affording home to nonconformity as is possible to imagine. That Dissent seeded deep into Welsh soil, however, owed much to conditions where a semi 'peasantry' lived under the sufferance of a landowner, and, when no longer wanted, a landless worker had to move with little prospect of anything but further hardship and distress. A key to the change of religious allegiance was the role of the Established Church as not only the official religious body but as a secular master, foremost among the landowners on whose decisions even the very life or livelihood of a person might depend. It was this division of landlord on the one side, and tenant farmer and landless labourer on the other that encouraged affiliation to a religious culture that was to become so much the hallmark of nineteenth-century Wales.

The Methodist Revivals of the mid-eighteenth century had repercussions far beyond the doctrinal religious. In fact, the remarkable growth in religious observance was not confined to Methodism, rather spreading across the denominations of Old Dissent and even the Established Church. The statistics for Chapel attendance are remarkable in themselves, but it is the less quantifiable spread of a Nonconformist culture that was the real effect. Here we must move beyond the Chapel service to the closely related history of learning and education. Before the nineteenth century, it is safe to say that aside from the small numbers taken into Choir or Grammar Schools, learning was informal, conducted through a passing on of knowledge and skills. The traditions of poets, storytellers, folklore, as well as wisdom in matters ranging from the treatment of sickness to the tending of crops, was not separated out as a compartmentalised 'education' but was simply part of the general learning of a people. Yet nearly all this knowledge was transmitted from generation to generation orally. It was a feature of Welsh society in the later eighteenth century that concerned literate, and mainly English, observers. It was at this point that language, learning, religion and the take up of Methodism, met. A central figure was Griffith Jones. His plan was for a continuous process of 'circulating schools', which would not depend on any fixed structure, either in terms of building or people, but would reside in a village or community for a period of weeks, during which time classes for children and adults would occur. Success was to be realisable because the teaching and learning would be in the language of the population, and there is little doubt that the circulating schools were historically significant in enabling Cymraeg to be read by a much greater number of persons than before. The increase in the numbers attending chapel over the one hundred and fifty years after the circulating schools, and the part played by chapels in enhancing a sense of national identity, forms then one of the structural features in the history of nineteenth-century Wales.

As a land-owning class found an anglicised identity to be to their advantage, taking on the language and religion of the powerful neighbours into which they sought to assimilate, so it found itself outside a nation rediscovering itself. A distinctly Welsh 'middling sort' was coming into being, and however much it lacked in number, it more than made up for by industriousness. If rural unrest was a marker of one kind of newfound confidence, then the flowering of literary and cultural periodicals in both Cymraeg and English was another. It would be a mistake to imagine a sudden conversion on the part of even a substantial percentage of the population to literary matters and they remained a minority concern, yet the appearance of the magazines was significant, marking as they did a resurgent national consciousness among a new class.

With this deep cultural change moving through Wales, went equally profound demographic and economic alteration. Before 1850, Wales boasted few large concentrations of people. Old trades such as the wool industry with its drovers pushing on their animals toward the midlands of England, remained, though these did not involve sufficient numbers of people to register more than local impact. The few market towns, though significant for trade and craft industries, were associated with the needs of a largely agricultural workforce and the geographic parameters for most of Wales was local, in terms of both the destination of produce and the import of materials. This might be understood as part cause for the underdevelopment of agriculture in much of the country. The lack of external influence and relative insularity of experience compounded the underinvestment by landowners, who were content to reap a surplus for little effort. From mid-century this began to change with the onset of new farming practices. If for landowners the incentive was increased income, for tenant farmers the incentive was the chance to improve the appalling standards of living commonly suffered.

Alongside agricultural changes came a substantial increase in the population in common with other parts of nineteenth-century Europe. What became distinctive, however, was a growing asymmetry whereby the increase happened almost entirely in a central and eastern part of the south while to the north and west the population decreased sharply due to migration into the newly industrialising area. Toward the end of the nineteenth century, this migration was hugely augmented by another into the south, this time from across the border in England and to a lesser degree, from Ireland and continental Europe. The movement into the coalfield and its metals industry at times outweighed that into London and meant that South Wales became perhaps the only area in Europe to gain population on such a scale. This inward flow of people was almost exclusive to Glamorgan and Monmouthshire, where in the early years the new iron towns acted as a frontier on which a new way of life and economy was being built. The push inside Wales, from mid and west of the country, was the chance to escape grinding poverty. That this may seem an odd claim is because the picture often offered from the nineteenth century is that of outside observers coming to the new industrial-based settlements from a place and class position which renders what they saw as something inexpressively hideous. Change the way of seeing, so that the perspective is that of generations of people who had struggled to survive in the face of landlord and farmer, and the 'hideous' iron town becomes a place of opportunity for a new life.

Plotting the increase in production of iron can serve

as a chart for the changing face of Cymru and its people. In 1796 total pig iron output in South Wales stood at 34.4 thousand tons, by 1855 this had grown to 840 thousand tons. The rise is dramatic and made towns like Merthyr synonymous with a new South Wales and indeed with Wales itself. The relative lack of increase after mid-century can be simply explained by the shift to steel, though in reality the geographical movement could be slight as towns such as Nantyglo altered from one metal to the next. Wider settlements around the town, and Ebbw Vale itself, have been the subject of an in-depth study by John Elliott, a central argument of which was that this eastern section of industrial South Wales was a substantial contributor to the region, even if it has received less attention than the central coal field of Glamorgan. Iron towns like Nantyglo and Abercarn were now industrial centres with the makeshift cottages put up directly by the iron companies, forming lines as terraces stretched out from the works.

At mid-nineteenth century, however, when output of pig iron slowed, industrial growth was far from exclusively southern and slate quarrying in the north remained significant. Slate was increasingly being used for houses and other building, and demand over the second half of the nineteenth century ensured significant profits, none more so than those accruing to Richard Pennant whose Penrhyn Estate accounted for a substantial part of total output. Pennant's infamy arose from the manner in which he controlled not merely the employment of workers but the life of families and communities whose cottages were parts of his estate, and from which they might be evicted. To the northeast, industry developed as part of the wider growth stretching beyond the Mersey and Manchester Ship Canal to cover much of northern England. Coal mining began in areas near Wrexham and in part served to fuel the demands of Lancashire, though the field remained limited in extent and output. In South Wales, however, the spectacular growth of the mining industry transformed the region. Between 1850 and 1890 the coalfield grew to become synonymous with the name 'South Wales'.

Around coal grew the sister industry of steel, as the new metal replaced iron, notably in the extraordinary development of railways that swept Britain, and on across the world. Steel production partly settled on the sites of iron, but the expansion in demand as the nineteenth century established the familiar pattern of city and industry, meant that much greater concentrations of productive capacity were needed. At the same time altering technology produced higher quality as well as tonnage. Together these changes precipitated the required increased concentrations of capital investment until only a few steel corporations accounted for the bulk of output in South Wales, extending their power by means of control of supplies of iron ore, shipping and rail lines. This pattern of increasing concentration of ownership would in time come to likewise typify the coal industry. In the mid-nineteenth century, however, the coal pit still represented something of an isolated venture, with single owners, discreet villages and labour-intensive extraction. A century later, this last feature was blamed for the economic weakness of the coalfield, but in the early years, it also reflected the human movement intent on escaping the poverty of rural life. A probable further attraction of the coal villages was the superior quality housing as compared with the earlier iron towns. A less attractive common experience was the near lordship over workers, which iron masters and early coal owners could exert by way of the company shop and truck system that allowed them to direct what people ate and had within their home.

The western coalfield was different in composition and appearance from that to the east. From the beginning, an outlet for anthracite coal was Swansea, the natural harbour formed by the sheltering Gower Peninsula, enabling cargo to be loaded in comparative safety. If tinplate and copper afforded a vital metals industry to the region and substantial export trade, anthracite coal rapidly established a quantitative domination that set the purpose and colour of the wider area. Pitheads were often located at existing villages, which meant new miners' housing was additional to that existing and so more likely to be of similar material and build, in contrast with deliberately built lines of housing for which no model existed. The pithead, however, still transformed a village, multiplying a population and imposing a new pattern of living. A further distinctive feature of the western field was the lower density of the pitheads. The process of increasing monopoly ownership of the coalfield could take different forms. Most obvious was simple accumulation of mines, until a majority of those in a given area were under single ownership. The Cambrian Combine ownership of mines in mid-Rhondda was an early and leading example of the trend. The geography of the majority of the coalfield, with its southern limit several miles from the sea, necessitated the building of a network of rail lines to move coal to the ports. The difference was again in the western coalfield, part of which stretched toward Swansea and the coast. Elsewhere rails were needed to move the volumes of coal from pithead to port, steel works or other place where it would be used or stored. Substantial increases in output came with the conversion to coal-fired steam ships along with the change by the Royal Navy from the 1840s on to coal power, thus increasing demand exponentially, with for some decades no obvious limit to the growth. The conversion itself stimulated greater trading of goods, so requiring more ship building, which in turn enticed more trading and movement of goods. Typical was the carrying of export coal from Newport, Cardiff, Barry and Swansea in one direction and the bringing in of foodstuffs or ores for steel manufacture as imports.

Yet to write the history only in terms of materials and trading is to leave out the movement, settling and life of people which lay at the heart of this physical transformation. It was the extraordinary migration of population that underpins the story of the industrialisation of the south, and at the same moment, the drastic effect on mid and North Wales as it suffered retardation with the loss of its young. Brinley Thomas carried out an in-depth examination of the migrations, calculating that between 1851 and 1911, 388,000 left rural Wales, while in the same period 320,000 moved into the coalfield. The population figures are extraordinary and warped the spread of people across the country so that by 1900 some four fifths of the population of Wales lived in the south-eastern belt.

In Wales, the 'industrial revolution' did not so much begin as erupt. The magnitude of the increases and changes in production that engulfed Wales were beyond prediction, design or rational control. What made the change in work and life so dynamic was the coupling of its extent with its speed. Gwyn Alf Williams pulled together a number of sources to provide figures, affecting population increase, migration, range of significant industries, output, and pre-eminence in global terms. Few of these figures were more startling than that for migration beyond Wales. In a complex equation, he compares exports of capital investment with migration. In the second half of the nineteenth century, the prime receiver of capital investments from the UK was the United States of America. Migration from England, Scotland and Ireland, like the rest of Europe, was broadly in line with flows of money, each increasing together and declining when domestic investment provided more jobs at home. In contrast, Wales witnessed only small emigration to the United States, and in fact experienced a continued net immigration through the 1880s and beyond into the twentieth century. Put in the manner of this cold calculation the history may be made abstract, but the reality it represents was the transformation both of Wales as a country and in the experience of its people. Raymond Williams grapples with this rupture between the two ways of representing a past near the start of *Border Country* in the figure of the young Matthew Price. An economic historian, his research has stalled as he finds the tools that his training has provided do not meet the problem he is addressing. He is travelling home on a London bus, and it is perhaps the narrator's voice we are hearing

It is a problem of measurement, of the means of measurement, he had come to tell himself. But the reality which this phrase offered to interpret was, he could see, more disturbing. He was working on population movements into the Welsh mining valleys in the middle decades of the nineteenth century. But I have moved myself he objected, and what is it really I must measure? The techniques I have learned have the solidity and precision of ice-cubes, while a given temperature is maintained. But it is the temperature I can't really maintain; the door of the box keeps flying open. It's hardly a population movement from Glynmawr to London, but a change of substance, as it must also have been for them, when they left their villages. And the ways of measuring this are not only outside my discipline. They are somewhere else altogether, that I can feel but not handle, touch but not grasp. To nearest hundred, or to any usable percentage, my single figure is indifferent, but it is not only a relevant figure: without it, the change can't be measured at all. The man on the bus, the man in the street, but I am Price from Glynmawr, and here, understandably, that means very little. You get it through Gwenton. Yes, they say the gateway of Wales. Yes, border country.

From the 1870s, the movement Matthew was measuring had become a flood as people left mid and west Wales travelling east and south. The figures were astonishing. As indicated near the start of the chapter, the demography of Wales underwent a peculiar change, with a vastly accelerated population rise due to increased life span, migration into the coalfield area and the coastal ports, and then a further inward migration from England, Ireland and beyond, also nearly all into South Wales. The two counties of Glamorgan and Monmouthshire received inflows of people far beyond that of anything comparable in Scotland or England. Drawing an analogy with the United States of America, the period has been called 'The Frontier Years'. Such an image may be appropriate, starting with iron and continuing with coal and steel, the building of South Wales consisted of villages and towns centred on single industries and common experiences that went beyond production to consumption with a truck shop and a payment system that forced workers to buy at this company store. There was nothing here of the garden suburb attempted by Quaker chocolate masters, Bourneville and Cadbury. More often, the early metal workers' and miners' houses were utilitarian in the extreme, a single cold tap proving the only source of water which itself was likely to come via a roughly laid pipe system from a supply near to hand. The accommodation of two-storey buildings could serve two households, one up one down. A shift pattern that could consist of three workings, 14.00 to 22.00, 22.00 to 06.00 and 06.00 to 14.00, negated the possibility of a single house ever having more than a few hours between the bodily cleaning of one shift of miners and the next. Between these hours women and girls took the strain of washing and drying the dust-ridden clothes of father, husband, brother or son.

The results were catastrophic for health, as a study by Steven Thompson of the central coalfield has demonstrated. *Unemployment, poverty and health in interwar South Wales* centres on the depression from the 1920s. Thompson's argument is that statistics for illness and death should not be too quickly attributed to seemingly obvious causes such as unemployment and intensified poverty, when morbidity and mortality rates are more intelligible if located in a number of socio-economic and cultural variables. What here is significant in Thompson's study is the reality where mortality and morbidity rates were already of such appalling levels in the coalfield, as compared with figures generally for the UK, that the long-term depression did not make them markedly worse. This said, Thompson claims that young pregnant women showed greater susceptibility to death especially if shorter-term strains intensified those which poverty imposed. In a related vein, Dai Smith has written of the atrocious level of infant mortality in the coalfield districts of Glamorgan, which, measured over time, were possibly higher than in any other part of Britain.

Inside this greater sociological picture lay a human story; the transformation that came as people brought forward their known means of living to make a new way of life that would in time produce not just coal and steel but culture and as Gwyn Alf Williams has termed it, the first

'Welsh Working Class'. The formation of a recognisable working class was arguably delayed as compared with parts of England, for reasons of inadequate internal transport and communications, but also by the distribution of population and industry. The main lines of transport at least were built, Gwyn Alf Williams argued, less for the benefit of those whose communities the railway passed through than to move English tourists and travellers across the intervening country to North Wales and the west coast. Communications is a theme closely associated with Raymond Williams, and the problems of geography and connections affecting rural Wales and its people was perhaps best addressed in *Fight for Manod*. Written parallel with *The Country and the City*, where the fundamental change in relations with the land are addressed historically, the novel captures the contradictions of taking forward a way of life so that it could grow and flourish where it is yet remain in the control of the people whose future was threatened with either extinction or exploitation.

In South Wales though, a negative account tells only half the story. The simple facts were that the newly industrialising area offered both higher wages and better housing than rural agricultural life. It is perhaps always easy to recognise poverty in urban environments because of the concentration of people, yet rural poverty had been a circumstance for much of the nineteenth century. The reasons are perhaps obvious: the limitations to transport and communications caused by the mountainous geography of the country, concentration of land ownership in estates, rendering working of the land an activity carried on by tenant farmers, and finally, only sporadic collective action to improve conditions on the part of farmer or labourer. From the mid-nineteenth century, the situation rapidly changed as estate owners through their control of parliament were able to pass law enabling the enclosing of land, which, followed by drainage and other measures, rapidly increased the productivity of farming. John Davies comments that from mid-nineteenth century periodicals began to be circulated through agricultural societies that grew rapidly in popularity, so that shortly each county had its own network disseminating ideas for how land might be better utilised.

The other side to enclosures was the potential pauperisation of those living on the commons. The previously free use of the land to build shacks and catch food suddenly becoming subject to rent payable to an owner where before none existed. Davies cites the clearances being particularly harshly carried out at Cardiff Heath by the Bute family who by parliamentary act had gained ownership. If people escaped the levels of brutality meted out in the violent Highland clearances of Scotland, the results were similar – landless people with little prospect of regular work, atrocious often temporary housing, they came to form what from the later nineteenth century was referred to as a landless proletariat owning only their own labour; the necessary supply for industrial capitalism to achieve take-off.

If this was the 'push' factor in driving people toward the metal and coal production of South Wales, then the 'pull' was the prospect of regular work and higher pay. In an imaginative scene in his novel *Black Parade* (2009), Jack Jones depicts the arrival and reception of newcomers to the industrial furnace that was Merthyr:

> 'Could you tell me how to get to Bethesda Street, please?'
>
> 'Huh?' grunted Glyn aggressively.
>
> The Stranger repeated what he had said.
>
> Glyn looked him over suspiciously. Yes, he thought, another of these farm-joskins, hundreds of them were weekly flocking into the coalfield lured by the prospect of what seemed to them extraordinarily high wages...
>
> 'Humph. Where you from?'
>
> 'From Hereford way, I be.'
>
> 'Off a farm?'
>
> 'That's it Edwards. The Croft... maybe you know it?'
>
> Glyn, now beginning to thaw, shook his head. 'And been doing a bit of walking by the looks of you?'
>
> 'More'n a bit. I been movin' since daybreak.'
>
> 'Well you haven't much further to go till you get to Bethesda Street.'...
>
> 'Do you think as I'll get me a job?'
>
> Glyn laughed shortly. 'What's to stop you? You're big enough, God knows.'
>
> 'Lord I be glad to hear you say that. And where do you reckon'll be best place for I to start at?'
>
> 'Take your choice, stranger, take your choice, for there's plenty of places waiting for likes o' you.' He stopped to point away to the right, and went on wasting irony: 'Up there to the seven Dowlais pits – but maybe they'll be a

bit far for you to travel to and fro night and morning, so p'raps you'd better start in one or other of those six pits across there. Them's the Cyfarthfa collieries, owned by Crawshay Brothers.'

'I think Amos said 'e works in one o' them.'

'Then down there to the left there's another six pits belonging to the Hills Plymouth Company.'

Merthyr was the largest town in Wales and from it on through the Rhondda, eastward to the edge of the coalfield, roughly north of Newport, and westward to the anthracite field ending near Caerfyrddin (Carmarthen) spread an industrial culture. Merthyr's early expansion was as an iron town, and John Davies offers a graft which shows that in 1840 some 120,000 tons of the material were coming from the Cyfarthfa, Penydarren, Dowlais and Plymouth ironworks located in the area. In *The Merthyr Rising*, Gwyn Alf Williams graphically recounts Merthyr's turbulent history, witnessing in 1831 an uprising that was to cost more lives than the massacre at Peterloo, Manchester in 1819. The executioners on this occasion were the Argyll and Sutherland Highlanders and many may have noticed the irony that troops named after the Scottish Highlands should put down a Welsh uprising, given the former place's history of insurrection. The soldiers were sent for, following a march several thousand strong, demonstrating a raised political consciousness, made all the sharper with the subsequent hanging of Dic Penderyn. Later, Merthyr was to express its advanced political beliefs through the election of the Radical Liberal MP Henry Richard unseating the incumbent Tory. Later still in 1900, Keir Hardie became the MP so establishing an Independent Labour Party presence in the coalfield and inspiring the turn toward Labour as miners began to switch allegiance from their tradition of Liberalism.

Keir Hardie aligns with changes that were transforming South Wales, where the shift from Liberal to Labour could be measured by the rise and direction of the South Wales Miners Federation. The Fed, as it was commonly known, started in 1898, following the miners' defeat in a struggle against their 'sliding-scale' system of payment used by the majority of pit owners. The scale linked wages with the price of coal and consequently with the vagaries of a fluctuating market. The miners' demand was for the establishing of a minimum wage, while the mine owners sought to lower wages in accord with their sliding scale to bring, as they saw it, wages into line with prices. Following the dispute, which caused much hardship for miners and families, the men were forced back to work on the lower wages, but in the same year formed The Fed, electing as President, Rhondda's William Abraham or Mabon as he was called by his bardic name.

Chris Williams' *Democratic Rhondda* is a detailed account of how Liberal-controlled Rhondda gradually and then suddenly changed to Labour. Chris Williams' study is an interweaving of a communal network, with those serving as Fed officials, Poor Law Guardians and Labour Councillors being simply part of a wider, less formal, common effort to improve a way of life. It is beyond the present chapter to trace the moves in voting and elected representatives, but it was an inexorable process, the First World War acting as something of a watershed, after which a Liberal political Party ceased to exert a significant influence in South Wales. It was a political situation that played a factor in the early life of Raymond (Jim) Williams, and it is to that we now turn. Pandy has been superbly discussed in Dai Smith's biography, as has Abergavenny where he attended Grammar School, and made the first step of his movement away from home. Here we limit ourselves to how the long history recorded above took substance for him at a very young age in the form of the 1926 miners' strike and lockout.

Pandy is not a nucleated village typical of southern England where the centre is often the Parish Church. It is a straggle of houses, farmsteads, the odd inn and two chapels. Zoar Baptist Chapel (1837) and Hope Calvinist Methodist Presbyterian Chapel (1866) sit opposite each other, each with a graveyard bearing testament to Pandy's people. Farmers of the area were overwhelmingly nonconformist and more Baptist than Presbyterian. Raymond's own family, however, were split between chapel and Church. We know he attended chapel as a younger child, under the influence of a grandmother (probably Gwen's mother) who stayed with the family. Later, however, Raymond attended the Church at Llanfihangel Crucorney as too did his father despite Raymond's claim of Harry's hostility to religion. Despite decades of previous struggles, an effect of which had been to make the Liberal Party an overwhelming political force across Wales, Disestablishment of the Church did not happen until 1920. The Act had in fact been passed in 1914, but putting it into practice was delayed by war. Dai Smith has discussed in his biography the support given Jim by Rev. Hughes of St Michael's Church at Llanfihangel Crucorney, and the transfer of that activity into the character of Rev. Pugh of *Border Country* and even ventured he was 'perhaps, in another guise, Will, Jim or Raymond himself'. It is worth mentioning how later in the 1950s, Raymond took his children to hear Rev. Hughes, and of how he pleaded Christian pacifism in his hearing when effectively refusing recall to the army at the time of the Korean War. It may interest some future researcher to unravel further if they can, this peculiar strand of Raymond's life, but here we must leave it that whatever the tensions in his family over religious affiliation, they did not result in Nonconformity being a part of Raymond Williams. Instead, perhaps, we might recognise in Williams something of a respect for the Established (Anglican) Church as it appears sporadically in a passage in *Border Country*. The Rev. Pugh is trying to explain to a young Matthew something of the Church he, in a Welsh village, represents in the manner of an 'outpost'. The image Pugh presents is of the Church as a network; the Rev. Pugh is an outpost of a structure that stretches back across the border to 'the cathedrals, the universities' … 'institutions' that constitute a history.

Built across the middle third of the nineteenth century, Zoar and Hope bear witness to the history of Pandy for much of the period discussed in this chapter. Standing now for the families who made the village, Zoar's graveyard contains the name Tranter several times, while at Hope, Parry is prominent. The two buildings stand between the river Honddu and the old road that now serves more for walking while a new road carries all else. Harry Williams was Branch Secretary for the local Labour Party, member of the National Union of Railwaymen and Parish Councillor. As such he epitomised some of what has been discussed earlier, a figure who lived and worked across activities that together meant engagement as part of a community and a wider society. The two words would always feature in Raymond's writing; in *Border Country*, community could be lived through beehive and bowling green, society through railway and signal-box telephone.

Language was a means by which Williams worked through his definition of community and society, and *Keywords* and the Introduction to *Culture and Society* are two places where this is openly so. The ideas contained in a more formal sociological distinction indicated by Gemeinschaft and Gesellschaft may have been part of a shift from English critic to continental theorist. Elsewhere, language could be a part of the action, as when Morgan and Harry are talking at a change of shift in the signal box. The moment is the hours ahead of the General Strike and preparation is needed:

> Harry stood re-reading the telegrams, above the low fire.
> 'General Strike then, is it?'
> 'Aye', Morgan said. 'And about time.'

Harry turned and took off his coat. 'All right,' he said. 'It's straightforward enough for us.'

'So long as we know what we're doing,' Morgan said...

Harry rubbed his hand over his face. 'We're with the miners, isn't it?'

'Aye, but we're with them why? Because we're the working class, Harry, united for common action. The miners are fighting their own battle against the employers. We're not mind. We're not fighting the companies, we're fighting the government.'

'The country they said,' Harry answered, half to himself...

'The country Harry! We're the country. And mind you if we come out let's realise it's that we're saying. We're saying that we're the country, we're the power, we the working class are defying the bosses' government, going on to build our own social system.'

'I don't know about that,' Harry said...

'I'll stand by the miners, if it comes to it.'

Morgan looked at him doubtfully, and then threw up his hands.

'If that's all it is mun, we shall lose. We're out for power, power in our own hands.'

Harry walked to the far end of the box.

'Shall we be all out here?' he asked, staring out into the darkness down the line.

'If I know anything about it, we shall.'

'Meredith?'

'You leave Meredith to me.'

'Aye, only Jack's a funny chap mind. Don't go talking to him about the working class and power and that.'

'Why not?' Morgan asked. 'He's a worker isn't he?'

Harry hesitated, and then looked round the box.

'Aye, only it's not the way we talk, so watch him.'

Raymond Williams was born in 1921; the General Strike only five years later happened therefore at a still formative age as he recalled in a talk given at a Llafur day school in 1976. The experience of the station and its porters, platelayers, gangers and signalmen is captured in *Border Country*, where 'the greatest strike in working-class history' is held over while a bed of snaps are planted. That ordinariness though, is key. Not alien, the strike required the discipline that ensured trains ran and the station function, to be administered toward another achievement, where ordinary working people brought into existence a society of their own making. In *Border Country*, that capacity is shown in the order and reasonableness with which the signal box is closed, and the chaos threatened by a signalman opposed to the strike is averted.

The subsequent lockout in the coalfield to the South required an extension of that organisation as food and essentials were carried down to the valleys in a van by Morgan who, after the strike and lockout ends, continues the run so becoming a regular supplier though now in a commercial form. The railway company's suspension of Harry, so that the box operated with one fewer, was similarly broken by organisation, albeit one involving the cussed figure of Meredith, who at the end of his shift, signs off, to leave a tanker marooned, with the comment that 'there's another signalman at home'. So it was, that Harry was reinstated. Yet, for the young Will in the novel, the experience of the punishment handed down in reaction to the strike, and his father's lay-off, became a cornerstone for Matthew's adult thinking. Raymond Williams, remembering this fifty years later in 1976, recounted some of that past bringing out the significance of the moment of working-class capacity for organising and the consciousness thereby realised.

Yet what comes through in these accounts of Williams' is that events, of which 1926 was unusually significant, do not occur in isolation and cannot, viewed separately, be fully understood. Rather, what happened was made possible by a longer history. What comes through is the lack of crisis. The needs at Pandy station in the strike were met with the same measured approach as they had been before; only now, the actions were those of labour transferred from the service of the company to instructions from elsewhere. Yet, there was also an autonomy and self-discipline made possible by local experience. The peculiar mix of rural and industrial, whereby for at least a generation people had worked on the land in field and under it in mine, according to season and need, continued. If the station with its physical connections, blast furnace and coal mine to southwest, manufacture to east brought to the village the history of industrial revolution, then the tending of crop in garden and field brought the history of agriculture and rural settlement. In *Border Country*, we can see a pattern where, when the one no longer requires the time, the other may be given greater labour.

1926 has been used here for its significance in Raymond Williams, as well as in the wider history of Wales. What made his experience, whether as a child or later in the answers he gained from his father and the accounts that appeared in print, was the transformation of Wales over the previous two hundred years. Here an emphasis has been given to the cultural creativity from that past. What was taken forward from Dissent was not so much doctrine as the vitality of people. Dissent served as channel for creativity, the Chapel building, the array of groups and activities continued through each week, and the festival marking occasion and season. Then as new patterns of work were learned in mine, mill and home, and when the production of those new places expanded to make possible alternative means of realising life in dance hall, sports field and theatre, different creative entertainment became possible. The concentration in village and town, meant movement away from Chapel and afforded an energy for which miners' institutes, libraries and halls served as a means of expression.

Desires for learning over the nineteenth century have already been illustrated. However, the greater concentrations of people that went to making the urban landscape of South Wales brought with it changes. The learning of basic skills that had sometimes been met through chapel was slowly replaced with an extension of state responsibility. As increasingly institutionalised education, notably through Elementary Schools, delivered primary skills to produce literate and numerate adults, so a potential population was created for more advanced learning. It was this advance that led to a peculiar circumstance in South Wales in the early twentieth century. The Workers Education Association (WEA) was formed through the efforts of varyingly progressive sympathisers responding to an in-depth examination of adult learning, published as *Oxford and Working-Class Education*. A core theme of the Report was encouragement of closer co-operation between existing higher institutions and working people. In South Wales, the efforts of the WEA were led by a small number of figures drawn from the professions and middle classes, concerned that too great a gulf existed between the 'cultured' and the worker, and that the latter could only benefit if introduced to at least the rudiments of higher learning, while simultaneously fearing a continued exclusion of the labourer from 'society' might leave space for the planting of subversive influences. The fear was not wrong, indeed from the class perspective of those who sought to teach this higher conciliatory wisdom, the growth of the South Wales Miners Federation could only have been a nightmare. Worse still, as well as the Fed, railway workers, steel makers and craft workers were forming unions. In the main, the new associations of workers were for no more than the pursuit of better pay and conditions, but in seeking to achieve these ends, there might come learning that pointed menacingly at the very heart of the present order of things.

In reality, the early attempts to form WEA classes met with limited success. Richard Lewis' forensic *Leaders and*

Teachers is an extended study of the politics of adult education in South Wales. The book provides detailed account of the motives, aspiration, means and achievements of those who laboured to make learning part of the normal experience of adults. Through the book, Richard Lewis pursues a central feature of the politics of adult learning in South Wales, the conflict between the WEA and Independent Working-Class Education.

Nowhere else in the British and Irish Isles was independent education more likely to succeed than South Wales, and to a remarkable degree, it did. That it declined in the years after World War Two was not perhaps because of any failing either in the content of classes or in the form adult learning took but because the wider culture was changing. Just as the chapels and Calvinist culture lost their hold to alternative means for cultural expression, so strenuous learning of history and economics was replaced with desire for literature. Reasons for the changes in classes have been little examined, but they were a matter of concern in WEA circles over a number of years. In the years 1910 to 1940, however, independent education challenged for the hearts and minds of miners, rail and metal workers across South Wales. The Fed, together with the National Union of Railwaymen, sustained a Central Labour College between 1909 and 1929. The Central College was a problematic institution, upsetting students and supporters, while its finances were always difficult. If in retrospect it is easy to damn the College as a drain of resources that could have more effectively been used in localities, the Central College nonetheless produced teachers who returned to their workplaces and enabled classes to be taught, with an emphasis on history and political economy, and, interestingly, the practical training of public speaking. Alongside the College and local classes, the National Council of Labour Colleges provided postal courses that groups of workers could use to their own ends. Much of all this originated before 1914 with The Plebs League, a slightly ambiguous and loose collection of activists, based around a paper of the name, but beyond that encouraging and supporting classes and courses wherever they occurred. In South Wales, the Rhondda was before 1920 replete with independent education classes, providing students for the Central College in London and enabling an educated leadership for The Fed.

If a detailed study of how adults in South Wales learned in the first half of the twentieth century has yet to be fully completed, the presence of the WEA alongside independent education meant classes were encouraged and where available, tutors were provided. Relations with Co-operative Societies, miners' institutes and the use of libraries enabled a culture where respect for reading and writing evolved, and so an educated cohort able to engage in wide-ranging debate emerged. The scale of these achievements is perhaps understood if this learning is placed alongside those other skills performed through choirs, bands, drama and recitals, and beyond these the creation of a literature which captured a way of life that became a history.

The extraordinary rise in population in South Wales and its tight-knit communities enabled new forms of opposition.

Where earlier action has been sporadic as with Rebecca Riots and Scotch Cattle; The Fed was a steady amalgamating of workers mine by mine and valley by valley. A continuity that passed through each institutional form being created was a common culture that made the South Wales that Dai Smith has captured in his own episodic autobiography, *In The Frame*. 1926 may be recognised as an extraordinary moment in that history and its portrayal in autobiography, fiction and history bears witness to its deep effect in Welsh society, one that re-echoed decades later. If socially the strength of South Wales could be seen in the ability of The Fed to slowly recover after the lockout and keep miners still united, then, culturally, a significant witness of people was an outpouring of writing. Originating in the interwar years, the Welsh Industrial Novel can be celebrated for its impetus to create diverse writers and novels, but also styles and even forms of writing. Raymond Williams' acknowledgement of this rich vein of work came not only in his lecture, *The Welsh Industrial Novel*, but also in the Foreword for the 1986 edition of Gwyn Thomas' *All Things Betray Thee*, and elsewhere.

The interwar years are a suitable place to end this account of Wales, directed, as it has been to provide a long and partial history against which Raymond Williams might be understood. The significance of the border country within the historical transformation has been left aside, since that is addressed elsewhere.

In time, writing produced a literary expression that gave witness to a culture, a whole way of life. The Welsh industrial novel in particular was a means by which a people could offer a record of its own existence, and what had been the pressures and limits through which a society had been realised. Raymond Williams sought to move beyond the forms offered by that industrial novel, and *Border Country* was the achievement. Matthew Price, the economic historian of that novel, sets out to account for the population changes that had made modern Wales. The mature figure he has become in *The Fight for Manod*, mirrors perhaps Raymond Williams' own settlement to that history, though only in order to take it forward once more.

Raymond Williams
Border Country, 1960, Library of Wales, Parthian, 2006.
The Long Revolution, 1961, Parthian, 2011.
The Country and the City, 1973, Spokesman, 2011.
The Fight for Manod, 1979, Hogarth, 1988.
Who Speaks for Wales? Raymond Williams, edited Daniel Williams, UWP, 2003.

Other works
Kathryn Cooper, *Exodus from Cardiganshire*, UWP, 2011.
John Davies, *A History of Wales*, UWP/Allen Lane, 1993.
Hywel Francis and Sian Williams, *Do Miners Read Dickens?*, Parthian, 2013.
Glamorgan County History Vol. VI: Glamorgan Society 1780– 1980, Glamorgan County History Trust, 1988.
Glyn Jones, *The Dragon has Two Tongues*, 1968, revised edition edited Tony Brown, UWP, 2001.
Ieuan Gwynedd Jones, *Communities: Essays in the Social History of Victorian Wales*, Gomer Press, 1987.
Mid-Victorian Wales, UWP, 1992.
Jack Jones, *Black Parade*, Library of Wales, Parthian, 2009.
Richard Lewis, *Leaders and Teachers*, UWP, 1993.
Robert Pope, *Building Jerusalem*, UWP, 1998.
Dai Smith ed, *A People and a Proletariat*, Pluto, 1980.
Dai Smith, *Raymond Williams: A Warrior's Tale*, Parthian, 2008.
Dai Smith, *In the Frame: Memory in Society 1910–2010*, Parthian 2010.

Chris Williams, *Democratic Rhondda*, UWP, 1996.

Gwyn Thomas, *All Thing Betray Thee*, Library of Wales, Parthian, 2011.

Glanmor Williams, *Religion, Language and Nationality in Wales*, UWP, 1979.

Gwyn A. Williams, *The Merthyr Rising*, Croom Helm, 1978.

The Welsh in their history, Croom Helm, 1982.

When Was Wales?, 1985, Penguin, 1991.

3

Crossing the Border

Elizabeth Allen

'Why did he go to Cambridge?'

This was the first question posed from the audience at the 2008 Hay Book Festival launch of Dai Smith's biography of Raymond Williams. If we assume that the questioner had in mind the first move, in 1939 to take up a scholarship at Trinity, then it is a question easily answered; the headmaster at his Abergavenny grammar school recommended him. But it is a move repeated in 1945 to resume his studies at the end of his service in the Royal Artillery, and in 1961 to take up an appointment as a Lecturer in English and a Fellow of Jesus. A move too which he presents as without agency on his own part. As he writes in the 1977 essay 'My Cambridge', 'In each of the three periods, I didn't ask or apply to come here.' This sense of manipulation is enacted in his novel *Loyalties*, published in 1985, where for Gwyn Price the move from the mining village of Danycapel to a

Cambridge college is less a personal decision and more a kidnapping, textually he is absent from his own interview.

The relation between Cambridge and Wales is crucial to the value system of Williams' work and it is important to recognise both the simple binary of hostility and loyalty which marks that relation and the more complex emotions which underpin it. It is an opposition of values established and reiterated throughout his writings, in fiction and non-fiction. Yet the content of the opposition is not stable, particularly where the 'Wales' values are concerned, and it is the complexities, and their importance for the way these inform and structure his writing, which will be explored here and in chapter five. One term, which can be read both as literal and metaphorical, persists: the importance of the 'border' and the anxieties invoked in its crossing. But where is this border marked? While Williams' writing demonstrates an intense consciousness of the spatial, and journeys across England, to and from the border country, structure the lives of his fictional characters, those journeys always signify other frontiers to be confronted and negotiated: between the different allegiances of the adult and the child, the personal and the collective, between linguistic practices.

The sharpest contrasts which Williams identifies, and to which he accords his most severely judgemental terms, are framed by his specific experiences of the population of Cambridge and of the community of his childhood and adolescence in Pandy. Against the world of the village where, as he writes in the 1958 essay 'Culture is Ordinary', 'An interest in learning or the arts is simple, pleasant and natural', he sets the Cambridge 'teashop' where people who were not 'particularly learned' and 'practised few arts' appropriated 'culture' for themselves by virtue of 'trivial differences of behaviour, their trivial variations of speech habit.' The making of this challenge to the meaning and ownership of culture, perhaps the central tenet of belief for Williams, is the grounds on which Stuart Hall declares his 'effective affinities' with Williams. Hall writes that, despite the 'tremendous differences… in temperament, character, background, ages and formation' he felt 'close' to him in their similar response to the institutions which were at the very centre of the dominant cultural system: Oxbridge. The pretensions of Oxbridge to appropriate 'culture' must be challenged.

The essay for the *My Cambridge* collection was written twenty years later. Here Williams excoriates the class 'which has dominated Cambridge' as smugly perceiving itself as 'well-mannered, polite, sensitive', congratulating itself on 'its taste and sensibility', its 'poise and tone', when it is in practice 'extraordinarily coarse, pushing, name-ridden.' He denies hotly that to respond thus is to demonstrate 'class-envy, class-resentment.' How, he asks could anyone 'fortunate enough to grow up in a good home, in a genuinely well-mannered and sensitive community… for a moment envy these loud, competitive and deprived people?' While, at the time of writing, he has spent eighteen years in the university, it has always felt to him 'temporary.' The opening sentence of the essay rejects the place and the purpose of the book designed to celebrate it, 'It was not my Cambridge.'

It is significant that the contrasts made in these essays written at very different stages in his life are drawn not in terms of national cultures but of two highly specific social groups. That Wales was not on the agenda in his early writings he explains to his interlocutors in *Politics and Letters* as a 'revulsion against what I saw and still see as the narrowness of Welsh Nonconformism'. In 'Culture is Ordinary', where he writes so movingly of the respect for learning and poetry felt among 'the scattered white houses' of his childhood, his silence on Wales is profound. The essay traces a bus journey from Hereford into the Black Mountains and the industrial valleys of south-east Wales. As the bus moves from fertile agricultural land to relatively untamed country, there is an intense consciousness of movements, physical and social, across geological, geographical and educational borders. But the other border which the bus has crossed, from English Herefordshire into Wales, is erased. This 'rejection of my Welshness', says Williams, 'I did not work through until well into my thirties.' The motive factor here is significant. The change occurred, 'When I began to read the history and understand it.' The narrative to which he could adhere was not that of the glories of the ancient Welsh princes which, he says, made him 'throw up' as 'it had nothing to do with us.' It was, rather, the account of the shifting power relations which had marked the land and the changing populations: the account of a past which suggested a possible future. Crucially, it was also the sense of a literary history which would form an important element in the way in which he positioned himself.

His relation to Welsh literature, and to Welsh literature in English, is a complex one which acknowledges virtues, identifies issues specific to Welsh writing in English and understands the situation of his own writing practices as problematic. His position needs to be read in the context both of his fraught relations to a politics of form which consumed the literary Establishment from the Second World War onwards, and of his response to different aspects of literary tradition on Wales. His engagement with Welsh literature is highly specific. The contention that Welsh culture and literature are intimately and necessarily bound to the use of the Welsh language does not appear to register strongly in most of Williams' writing, although in *Politics and Letters* he does comment on the post-Industrial Revolution 'elimination' of Welsh in the border areas as one tactic of the Anglicisation that was a conscious hegemonic strategy. A rather stronger later response to the language question is identified by Ned Thomas in a recent edition of *Planet: the Welsh Internationalist* where he records Williams' response to the extra-mural class on Williams' work run in Welsh, 'The language is, of course, absolutely central.' The consistent emphasis in his critical writing is the argument that 'Welsh literature in English' is distinct from English literature in that 'its writers have been shaped by Welsh culture, history, landscape and language.' He resists, however, the practice of what he calls 'the extreme verbal exuberance of the "Welsh style".'

Williams was always exercised by the political dimensions of linguistic choice. 'Style', he argues in his introduction in

English Prose, 'is inseparable from the substance of the ideas and feelings expressed' and from the relationship between a writer and his intended readers or listeners. The willed austerity of *Border Country,* consciously distanced from the intoxicating hyperbole of Gwyn Thomas or the violent verbal energy of the stories of Caradoc Evans, demonstrates a choice which distances him from important elements of the Welsh fictional tradition. Terry Eagleton's comments on the strategies adopted by Irish writers of the Celtic Revival period before political independence, of a 'rollicking rhetoric' whereby they 'tried to compensate for their political marginality with verbal brio, defiantly asserting their cultural difference', are suggestive here. Whether for reasons of taste, an Anglicised education or long exile, Williams did not see the linguistic choices of a 'rollicking rhetoric' as available to him.

Suspicious of a Welsh style which, he believes, functions as 'a form of cultural subordination, the only – slightly degraded if subtle – way the Welsh could present themselves to an English audience', Williams nonetheless considers Gwyn Thomas' *All Things Betray Thee* as a 'remarkable creative achievement' and wrote the Foreword for the 1987 edition. His commentary in his essay 'The Welsh Industrial Novel' is illuminating not only for what he has to say about this particular novel but for what it suggests of the principles which produce his readings of other texts and his own fiction: the commitment to realism which was to put him at odds with so many in the last decades of his life. To position oneself as a Welsh writer was anyway to place oneself at the margins. The politics of form which dominated critical thinking from this time identified the Realist novel as essentially a conservative form. It was understood as seeking to effect 'closure' of a single and uniform ideological position by the use of a set of hierarchised discourses, subjected to a controlling 'truth-voice'. Its other tactic was claimed to be an obscuring of the textual nature of the work, thereby naturalising and legitimating existing social structures and such concepts as 'human nature.'

Essentially Williams agrees with the assertion of Fredric Jameson, 'I assume... that all forms of aesthetic production consist in one way or another in the struggle with and for representation.' A double emphasis marks Williams' allegiance to realism: an admiration of what the realist tradition of the nineteenth and early twentieth century achieved and a belief that, as he writes in the lecture published as 'A Defence of Realism', it is a 'highly variable and complex term'. This belief is given perhaps its most explicit expression in a *Guardian* review of Solzhenitsyn's *The First Circle*. Identifying the 'fragmented' nature of the text, he writes that it is nevertheless, 'as different as anything could be from what is known in the west as experimental literature. It is a novel in the great realistic tradition, which has transformed itself to meet altered reality.' There is an important parallel in his reading of *All Things Betray Thee* as he recognises this novel's distance from the 'great tradition' of nineteenth-century realism, its 'reaching for new perspectives and new forms' as being precisely the grounds on which it may claim to be, like *The First Circle*, in 'the great realistic tradition.' He begins by noting, 'Its mode is surprising… in its deliberate distance from the close identifications of the realist manner.' The mode is, he writes, 'Less representation – the common currency of fiction – than rehearsal and performance, a composition primarily governed by the rhythms of speech and song', appropriate to the central character of the travelling harpist. Not then, Realism as it is generally understood. Yet the achievement, as Williams understands it, is precisely in its 'commitments', its fidelity, being 'at once visionary and historic'.

The term 'visionary' is suggestive. Williams' category of realism was sufficiently capacious to contain not only *The First Circle* and *All Things Betray Thee* but, in the essay 'A Defence of Realism', the Ken Loach/Tony Garnett film, *The Big Flame*. This moves from what he terms 'a developed realist film', dealing with industrial action in the Liverpool Docks to 'a politically imagined possibility' which, he argues, can be categorised as realism since it is 'played out in realist terms.' He recognises that the hypothesised political action is 'perhaps inconsistent with the narrower definitions of reality', but that adjective already demonstrates his rejection of such definitions. It is, he goes on to say, an effective development.

It is useful in this context to look at Williams' sustained interest in the possibilities of the Utopian and science-fiction genre which began early in his career with a short piece published in 1956 in the Workers Education Association journal. Here, as in a 1978 essay on 'Utopia and Science Fiction', which appears in an abbreviated version in *Towards*

2000, utopian fiction and science fiction are linked in their relation to realism. Williams has commented that, although these forms appear to be linked by '*otherness*' as 'modes of desire or of warning in which a crucial emphasis is obtained by the element of discontinuity from ordinary realism', what is most important 'is the continuity, the implied continuity. Which the form is intended to embody.' His most extended discussion of a particular text is of Ursula Le Guin's *The Dispossessed*, and it is interesting that Le Guin herself, in a *Guardian* review, asserts that 'science fiction is a mode of realism not of fantasy.' In this regard, it is a pity that there is no record of Williams' response to the Glyn Jones 1938 novella 'Born in Ystrad', where the Oxbridge-educated teacher protagonist, in a narrative shift into the stunningly surreal, becomes a leader in a failed socialist Welsh revolution. What is clear and consistent in his responses to such texts as *All Things Betray Thee, The First Circle, The Big Flame* and *The Dispossessed* is that he understands realism as a complex term, adherence to which demands from its practitioners a serious engagement. This was a challenge that he saw English critics and novelists, from different perspectives and over a period of decades, as failing to meet. In the fight for representation, it was not the realist form which he understood as the problem, rather, it was the ideological assumptions which had limited and continued to limit understanding of the scope of what should be represented.

The fifties had seen a backlash against modernism and experiment in the novel, a movement which sought to situate modernism as apolitical and even reactionary in opposition to a realism concerned with social progress. It was a debate marked by over-simplification and ill-defined terms. The 'experimental' novel's focus on the 'inner life' was understood as a retreat from history rather than, as Williams would later point out in 'Region and Class in the Novel', an emphasis constituted *by* history. The 'Realists', central among whom were C. P. Snow and William Cooper, identified an opposition between 'Man Alone', who rejects the turmoil and retreats into a solipsistic formalism, and 'Man in Society', determined to engage with quotidian social demands. Examination of Williams' writings on fiction more or less contemporary with this debate demonstrates that while he is, predictably, on the side of 'Man in Society' as the proper concern of novels, he redraws the terms of the debate. The more nuanced readings offered by *The Long Revolution*, published in 1961, engage with the relations between the individual and the collective, with the concepts of public and private, in ways which underpin his entire writing project, both fictional and non-fictional.

The crucial element is the 'balance' between the social and the personal. Society is not merely a 'background against which the personal relationships are studied, nor are the individuals merely illustrations of aspects of the way of life.' While he sees *The Rainbow* of D. H. Lawrence (1915) and Thomas Mann's *Magic Mountain* (1924) as measuring up to this ideal, no contemporary English novels approach it. In particular, the chapter 'Realism and the Contemporary Novel' rejects the claims of a number of writers then being promoted as offering new and exciting fictional models. Williams is dismissive of the 'personal' novel that has degenerated into a fiction which takes 'only one person seriously, but ordinarily very seriously indeed.' John Braine's *Room at the Top* is labelled as 'crudity and self-pity.' Novels featuring upwardly socially mobile young men attacking middle-class authority figures were then being hailed as 'progressive' and thirty years later Malcolm Bradbury would still read *Lucky Jim* as a 'class revolt.' Without naming Amis's novel, Williams roundly rejects any claims it might have to carry a socially progressive message: any real tension and shock, he writes, is displaced by the 'phantasy release of swearing on the telephone, giving a mock-lecture, finding a type-figure on which aggression can be concentrated.'

If the modes of Braine and Amis failed, it is still perhaps surprising to find Williams' later silence on writers with whom he might have been supposed to find some common cause, such as Doris Lessing, whose analysis of the colonial experience in the *Children of Violence* sequence was published between 1950 and 1968, or Margot Heinemann, whose *The Adventurers*, published in 1960, the same year as *Border Country*, is a committed – and critically and commercially successful – account of left-wing politics between 1943 and 1956, principally set in a Welsh mining community. But if Williams is negative or silent on English or metropolitan-based contemporary authors, he does later become more consciously aligned with a particular Welsh literary tradition, that of working-class fiction which seeks to represent 'fully developed class relations.' In a lecture given to the Robert

Tressell Society in 1982, he is still struggling with the practice of representing 'the class', so much more problematic a task as 'the class is a matter of consciousness... a matter of organization... a social reality and yet at the same time not necessarily a social reality which exists in anything like the same way a family does.' It is here that one finds the basis of his positive readings of Welsh novelists writing in English.

In *Politics and Letters,* he identifies the formation of this allegiance as occurring in the late sixties when: 'I began having many more contacts with Welsh writers and intellectuals, all highly political in the best traditions of the culture.' One of these was the historian Dai Smith who, in 'A Novel History', an account of the Welsh industrial novel, argues that the representation of this culture cannot be accomplished by a 'private' mode: this is 'a culture that requires politics in its art as well as its activity, for its social being to be articulate.' Williams agrees, Welsh writers 'cannot accept the English pressure towards a fiction of private lives. This is not because they do not know or value privacy, but because the painfully administered history of their own people teaches that the deepest humanity of the self is released by human involvement of a broader sweep.' Here Williams recognises a fictional tradition that engages with his writing practice and sense of the possibilities of realism in the later twentieth century.

The confrontational tone of the lecture 'Working-Class, Proletarian, Socialist: Problems in Some Welsh Novels' is very much that of a personal and ongoing engagement with problems of the representation of the invisible, and fictionally unrealised, wider system and with the situation of the writer who has moved out of the working class. The emphasis is on the negotiations necessary for the committed novelist in representing his (and in the context of Williams' account the personal pronoun is unavoidably male) class in its relation to the wider system. In this lecture and in the essay 'The Welsh Industrial Novel', Williams explores the difficulties of a form which if written from within a working-class community risks self-enclosure: 'The very intensity of the community... is the only and sufficient thing to write' and there can be no realisation of 'the wider system.' He finds the commitment of Lewis Jones's *Cwmardy* and *The Way We Live* 'inspiring', engages with the very different model of *All Things Betray Thee* which seeks to include 'the struggle in its most general form.' The emphasis on the continuing struggle for adequate representation and learning from 'our fathers, our comrades', however, is consistent.

The lecture ends with an analysis of the 'new problems within some new opportunities', which are relevant to the post-1950s. Here he identifies as the predominant working-class form 'the novel of working-class childhood and the move away from it.' Williams draws a distinction between the English and the Welsh novelists in their configuration of this move. It is, he says, 'From *Sons and Lovers* on, a significant English form. The working-class childhood is strongly written; the move away from it is given equal force. It is less common in Welsh writers.' In the lecture, he cites Gwyn Jones as 'sharing the same apparent trajectory' but insisting on 'the broader and persistent family experience.'

In the essay 'Region and Class in the Novel', he locates the Welsh rejection of a 'fiction of escape and flight' in the Welsh industrial novel more generically. It is in this context that one understands his own novel writing practice, 'I wrote *Border Country* and *Second Generation* against this pattern [of the move away being granted equal force]. I included the childhood and the mobility but making them interact with a persistent working-class life.'

Border Country, his first published novel, is the story of Matthew Price, a London-based academic, called back to Glynmawr, the Welsh border village of his boyhood, by the illness of his father, Harry, a railway signalman. Glynmawr is clearly based on Williams' own village of Pandy and the nearby market town of Gwenton, where Will attends the grammar school, in Abergavenny. The novel is structured by chapters alternating Matthew's visit and the narrative of Harry and Ellen from their arrival in the village as a young married couple to the time of Matthew's departure to study at Cambridge. The novel, with Harry's death in the penultimate chapter, is centrally concerned with the emotional and political unease that his life, and the values that it establishes, raise for his son. The character of Morgan Rosser, a fellow signalman and union activist frustrated by the failure of the 1926 General Strike, is the prototype of a character which will recur in Williams' novels, an articulate, politicised man or woman incapable of emotional or sexual fidelity or, in later models, incapable too of becoming rooted, of settling. The chapter dealing with the strike and its aftermath demonstrates clearly the way in which, specifically through the action of the railwaymen in supporting the striking miners who are represented in the text by 'the glow of the steel furnace' in the evening sky, the culturally intimate community of Glynmawr is, materially, through the lines of the railway, the telephone wires that connect its signal box with boxes west and east, the collection and transport of food, and the abstract idea of class solidarity, part of a 'wider system.' The General Strike itself, of course, demonstrates what Williams in his lecture on *The Ragged-Arsed Philanthropists* called one of 'those very articulate and organized moments' when a class is shown as 'operating collectively', offering the novelist the opportunity to represent class interests relationally. Yet the achievement of the form proper for *Border Country* clearly presented Williams with an enormous challenge.

The challenge that he faces in the representation of the move away, with the necessity to avoid the sense merely of 'escape and flight', and the strategy which he adopts to meet this challenge, is clearly signalled by the chapter organisation. Equally clear in *Border Country*, however, is the division signalled in the negotiation of that move. In his home village of Glynmawr Matthew was, and continues to be, known as Will, a split that mirrors Williams' own double naming:

> All the people who knew me until I was eighteen called me Jim. I adopted my legal name Raymond at university. The two names in the novel, and my own experience, point up the problems of being two persons to know, and of negotiating between two different worlds.

The spatial shift across the border is marked by name, and by linguistic register. When in chapter one the man, to whom we have been introduced in the opening pages set in London as Matthew, arrives by train at the station in Gwenton, the market town where he attended the grammar school, he is greeted by Morgan Rosser as 'Will' and it takes the time of the drive to the village, mostly in silence for 'it to be easy at last' Matthew falls back into the speech patterns of his boyhood and Morgan can be comfortable again in the presence of Will. Nevertheless, the meanings ascribed to the spaces travelled and the borders crossed remain complex. The move away is understood as at once necessary, disabling and disloyal. It is necessary in that it is part of the formative historical experience for some of Williams' generation, yet it is also part of a personal history, and at this level triggers an anxiety of exile and guilt which establishes the pattern of Williams' fiction. What, then, are the borders which have been crossed and which evoke pain? Glynmawr lies 'only three miles away' from the place where the 'border river curved in towards the village': the Welsh–English border is clearly invoked in the novel's title. Yet the power of the border, and the potential pain of the act of crossing that border, lies elsewhere.

When Harry and Ellen arrive in Glynmawr, we are told that this is not 'strange country' to them. They knew each other as children, Harry having been born in Llangattock 'only seven miles north-west, and Ellen in Peterstone, three miles farther north.' The villages, though, are divided by a river and 'that is the border with England.' Their accents mark the boundary, as 'in Peterstone, the folk speak with the slow, rich Herefordshire tongue' and this 'could still be heard in Ellen.' This is 'a frontier crossed in the breath.' Yet the 'quick Welsh accent' on the Welsh side of the divide is itself different, 'less sharp, less edged', than the accent of the valleys. Later, when Matthew meets the family doctor, Evans, he hears 'a Welsh voice, but very different from the Glynmawr accent: smoother, with narrower vowels – persuasive, in every rhythm, ingratiating even. Whereas here the rhythm is an unfinished truculence.' There is no sense here of a powerful binary opposition. In one episode, when Harry is driven by Morgan Rosser to drink in the Silver Fox pub, the importance of the border is simply that the Fox, lying on the English side of the river, can offer its customers cider on a Sunday, while pubs on the Welsh side are 'dry.' Williams uses this incident for a dig at Nonconformist hypocrisy. 'It's quiet tonight', Harry remarks, to which the landlord responds, 'Aye. See a few more after chapel.' This is a political border lightly drawn.

The dominant cultural practices encountered in the novel are indeed Welsh: the importance of the chapels serving as landmarks; the history taught at the village school being the highly coloured narration of the death of 'the good Gruffydd ap Llewellyn, the head and shield of the Cymri'; the detailed and powerfully imagined account of the village Eisteddfod. Yet each of these provokes ambivalent reactions in the boy Will, his response to the community experience of the Eisteddfod being particularly striking and constructed explicitly in terms of the crossing of a border other than the one marked by the river which divides his mother's from his father's village. As the conductor identifies each child performer by reference to an intricate web of family relationships: Elinor Watkins, the daughter of Mary Rees, 'Mary with red hair to her shoulders singing here where I am standing, eleven years old', who married 'John Watkins, the son of my very old friend John Watkins the Bridge', Will acknowledges that this 'ceremony of identification and memory' is 'centrally the meaning of life.' Yet he yearns to witness it destroyed, longing for 'some extraordinary blunder: the child given the wrong mother; the parents mixed up; bastardy and confusion flung across the valley by that compelling voice.' He continues to resist the pull of the celebration of the collective until as, in the evening session, the choirs begin, he recognises that 'it was no use at all even trying to stay separate.' The voices rise 'until you listening were the singing, and the border had been crossed.' This border, between Will's individual alienation and the pull of the communal ceremony, is rendered as far more powerful than the line on the map.

When, in *The English Novel*, Williams writes of the concept of 'border country', he understands this less as a geographical space and rather as 'that border country so many of us have been living in: between custom and education, between work and ideas, between love of place and an experience of change.' His subject here is Thomas Hardy and his re-construction of Hardy's experience in terms of his own fraught class insertion is a characteristic move. Another writer whom, in *The Country and the City*,

Williams elects as demonstrating affinities is Richard Jefferies, those affinities being constructed in such a way as to reinforce the identification of rural figures necessarily misread by the metropolitan centre. Jefferies he reads as a man with 'a lonely intensity', having powerful 'feelings for the physical world' but sensing that 'the working rural world' is 'decisively altering.' It is this Jefferies, whom he constructs by supplementing the autobiographical with the social history, and of whom Williams writes that he 'more than anyone' 'offers him a way of self-analysis.' This account of writers of a border land which is situated in historical and social, rather than national political terms, suggests very strongly the particular division of allegiance which explicitly drives *Border Country* and underpins Williams' writings and the complexities of his fiction, the relation of the Son and the Father.

It is not merely that, predictably, fathers and sons feature as characters, but that the protagonist plays the role of son rather than that of lover, husband or father. The Matthew of *Border Country* has a wife, Susan, and two sons but, although the novel encompasses his life from birth, the novel's structure conceals his acquiring of this 'new' family, with Susan making only fleeting appearances in the opening and closing pages. A rather different structural model in the later episodic *Loyalties* means that Gwyn Lewis moves between episodes from a Cambridge undergraduate to a position as a Civil Servant with a wife and daughter. His emotional crises and political choices are centred on his two father figures, his birth and adoptive fathers. *Loyalties* and *The Volunteers* also yield interesting examples of nakedly Oedipal aggression.

'His whole mind seemed a long dialogue with his father – a dialogue of anxiety and allegiance, of deep separation and deep love. Nothing could stop this dialogue. Nothing else seemed important.' Although Matthew identifies the relationship with his father as a 'dialogue', what the fiction offers, in *Border Country* and in the later novels, is not only a dialogue between generations but an emphasis on the need of the son to explain and to justify his move to that other world – to the world which can be identified as London or as Cambridge but is a world elsewhere. It is ironic that while Williams has been identified by a younger generation of critics as 'the Good Father', Williams' concern in his fiction is rather to construct himself, through those fictional protagonists with whom he might be in part identified, as the Good Son. To this end, his fiction employs a range of structural devices and enormous textual energies. The construction of Harry Price as father figure in *Border Country*, and the relationship of this figure to Williams' own father, Henry Joseph Williams, is therefore highly significant. The construction of the Good Son in this novel is structured around two sets of 'doubles': the Good and the Father, Harry Price and Morgan Rosser, and, explicitly, the 'personal' and the 'social' father. The negotiation of these relationships demonstrates the 'dangerous distance' involved in the border crossings.

Throughout *Border Country*, Matthew is shown as wrestling with the guilt of exile. To his mother he protests,

'I feel as if I'm being blamed. Blamed for something that is quite inevitable.' His journey, though, was the journey of his generation. To Morgan he explains,

> A part of a whole generation has had this. A personal father and that is one clear issue. But a father is more than a person, he's in fact a society, the thing you grew up into… We've been moved away and put into a different society. We keep the relationship but we don't take over the work. We have, you might say, a personal father but no social father.

In 'Tenses of the Imagination', Williams writes of 'the loved physical father' who 'in a time of exceptional social and especially educational mobility' could not take on the 'real father's functions, passing on knowledge and experience and judgements and values in this differently constituted and discontinuous social situation.' 'Loved' he may be but found wanting in the functions of a 'social father' he must be. It is thus Harry as a social father whom Matthew loses, but he does so in common with many of his generation. The subject of Matthew's own studies is 'population movements into the Welsh mining valleys in the middle decades of the mid-nineteenth century': these are migrations motivated by economic pressures and not by personal whim and rejection of paternal values. When the headmaster at Will's school raises the possibility of his trying for a university scholarship, it is the headmaster who is the more conscious of the implications of the plan, that this would mean moving into 'a quite different world.' Harry insists that it is part of a standard process, 'None of us is doing what our fathers are doing. None of us is living quite as they lived.' In their final conversation, now in the face of Matthew's contention that he has 'grown away', Harry reiterates his argument: 'How many ever live just like their fathers?' The pressure of this insight is maintained throughout the fiction, but there are moments when it does not serve wholly to contain the sense of guilt.

There are, unarguably, striking parallels between Williams' life and family and those of Matthew Price, and these have allowed some commentators on *Border Country* to elide Williams with Matthew and his father with Harry. The critic Laura Michele, for example, declares that the novel 'draws upon… his remembrances of the General Strike of 1926 as it is recalled time and time again in the novel through the voices and recollections of his father, Harry Price, and his friend Morgan Rosser'. It can be argued that Williams invites this elision, in his comments in the late interview 'The Practice of Possibility' that 'perhaps I explained [the crisis that came to me on the death of my father] partly in my novel *Border Country*.' Yet when, in the *Politics and Letters* interviews, he offers his account of the life and characteristics of Henry Joseph Williams, the man he constructs is not Harry Price. It is a part only of Harry Price and the absences and emphases are important.

His interviewers, allowing no weight to his cruel obduracy towards his young wife's wishes over their home and the naming of their son, have claimed that Harry is someone with 'a wholeness of character that commands an absolute respect' and that he is 'seen as a figure virtually without contradiction.' Williams responds that 'the character of Harry Price' was arrived at only after several re-writings and 'was not based on my own experience.' Harry, he says:

> is not my own father because a lot of him went into Morgan too. It would have been possible to combine his contradictory impulses in the same character. I tried that but in the end decided to separate them out by creating another character who represented the much more restless, critical and self-critical side of my father's nature.

While Williams here explains the split as simply a novelist's strategy, it has profound implications for the 'dialogue of anxiety and allegiance' and the choices made by the son. The father whom Williams describes in *Politics and Letters*, arrived in Pandy 'totally radicalised' by his experiences as a solider in the First World War and by his first post 'right down in the mining valleys which were very politicised, with a fairly advanced Socialist culture.' In this very different culture, he remains politically active as a member of the parish council and the village Labour Party branch. This, then, is the father whose 'contradictions' need to be 'separated' into the two figures whose often contending values structure the novel. Throughout the novel, Harry is identified with the positive virtues of settlement, loyalty to family and to class, integrity and wholeness. Positioned against him, structurally and in a number of set-piece dialogues, Morgan, the Union activist, who emotionally disturbed following the betrayals of the General Strike, becomes a successful businessman and Labour councillor. While Morgan is fluent, able to deploy the abstractions of political debate, Harry is quiet, practical and genuine. In a discussion about the railway workers' support for the miners in 1926, Morgan draws the distinction that the miners' argument is with the mining companies but the railway workers are 'fighting the government', and tries to explain to Harry the hegemonic move made by the Establishment in their use of the concept 'the country.' 'The country, Harry! We're the country!' Harry's terms, never articulated but implied in his simple assertion that he will 'stand by the miners if it comes to it', are those of an untheorised class loyalty. Although Morgan plays the role of an often sympathetic and persuasive advocate, Harry's values remain assured, and Morgan explicitly understands Harry's life as having put his own choices in question.

Morgan's business has expanded to include a jam-making factory in Gwenton and he has already made an offer to Harry to join him in the work, urging that his qualities would be ideal in buying fruit and other produce from the local farmers. In a late scene, Morgan invites the schoolboy Will to be a partner in the business, with the promise of 'getting ready when the time comes to take things over.' The offer may have been agreed with Eira; the story includes several references to more than friendship between her and Will and with his mother's approval. Will, readying himself for his university scholarship, declines the offer. After a scene in which Morgan initially declares himself 'insulted' by the rejection, an uneasy settlement is restored. Within him though, Will feels the importance of the incident, 'The quarrel has been only superficially about the job... This was a border defined, a border crossed. It felt like a parting, whatever might actually follow.' Thus Will is given a clear and significant choice, between leaving to make his own way in a presently uncertain future, or settling to a life with Eira and Morgan. When the former enters the room, it is to Eira that Will turns for direction, but their conversation is negated by Morgan and Harry.

Though a decision is reached, what might be registered is the choice that is not on offer. Harry Price's job and life are clearly not an available option for the young Will. Yet it is Williams' decision to divide the Father that may have erased this possibility. A father politically active and articulate would have offered a far stronger counter challenge to the university scholarship than Harry or Morgan individually, a challenge which would have needed to be acknowledged. While Williams' essays and speeches abound with acknowledgements of the educational work in the Welsh valleys in the early and mid-twentieth century, and his critical works offer examples of working-class heroes such as self-taught nineteenth-century historian Joseph Ashby, there is a significant absence in his fiction of the working-class activist defined not only in terms of commitment and integrity but also of an understanding of wider pressures. The novel having been constructed thus, Will must inevitably move into a world where he will be doing a job different from his father. He must become Matthew whose work on migration into the valleys in the nineteenth century, as described in the opening pages of the novel, has left an unease at the way in which he finds himself unable to measure the real substance of that movement, which he realises to have existed from experience of his own move.

In the final pages of *Border Country* Matthew, back in London, talks with Susan in terms intended to evoke both the literal and the psychological journeys he has made. There is a move towards resolution as Matthew declares that he can now measure the distance travelled and 'that is what matters.' It is this ability to measure, not going back, which means 'the end of exile.' In this final dialogue, Matthew refers to the first journey, the journey from Glynmawr to Cambridge, which was never his. Then, as at a number of points in the novel, he in his mind looks across at the mountain which, in *Border Country* and elsewhere in the fiction, is identified as the Holy Mountain. There was a strong tradition that the split summit which gives this mountain its highly distinctive shape was, like the Veil of the Temple, riven at the hour of the death of Christ, and local people still sometimes refer to it as the Holy Mountain, although now more often citing the ruined chapel near the summit as explanation for the name. However, on OS maps, and indeed on the map that appears in Williams' final novel sequence *People of the Black Mountains*, the mountain is given its official name of Skirrid Fawr. It has always to me seemed that it is this name, from the Welsh *Ysgyrid*, a derivation of *Ysgariad*, meaning divorce or separation, which serves better to represent Williams' relation to the various border countries in which he lived. But to be on the borders is not only a source of pain. The following novel, *Second Generation*, places one of its main protagonists, Peter Owen, on another summit in the Black Mountains, Hay Bluff, one which marks the border of Wales and England. Here he encounters 'a cancellation, an annihilation', the danger is extreme as the fragile boundaries of self threaten to disintegrate. To be 'at the margins', says Mary Douglas 'is to have been in contact with danger' and that 'danger lies in transitional states because danger is indefinable.' But if the individual survives the test, she goes on, 'to have been at the margins is to have been… at a source of power.'

Raymond Williams

'Culture is Ordinary', 1958, reprinted in *The Raymond Williams Reader*, edited John Higgins, Blackwell, 2001.

Border Country, 1960, Library of Wales, Parthian, 2006.

The Long Revolution, 1961, Parthian, 2011.

Second Generation, Chatto and Windus, 1964.

The Pelican Book of English Prose, Volume 2 ed. Penguin, 1969.

The English Novel from Dickens to Lawrence, Chatto and Windus, 1970.

The Country and the City, 1973, Spokesman, 2011.

Politics and Letters, 1979, Verso, 2015.

'Region and Class in the Novel', 'The Ragged-Arsed Philanthropists' and 'The Tenses of Imagination' in *Writing in Society*, Verso, 1984.

Loyalties, Chatto and Windus, 1985.

'The Practice of Possibility' in *Resources of Hope*, Verso, 1989.

'My Cambridge' and 'A Defence of Realism' in *What I Came to Say*, Hutchinson, 1989.

'Working-class, Proletarian, Socialist: Problems in Some Welsh Novels' in *Who Speaks for Wales? Raymond Williams*, edited Daniel Williams, UWP, 2003.

'Utopia and Science Fiction' and 'The Welsh Industrial Novel' in *Culture and Materialism*, Verso, 2005.

Other works

Mary Douglas, *Purity and Danger*, RKP, 1966

Terry Eagleton 'Mothering', *London Review of Books* 21:10, October 1999.

Stuart Hall 'Culture, Community, Nation' *Cultural Studies* 7:3, 1993.

Dai Smith 'A Novel History' in T. Curtis ed. *Wales: he Imagined Nation*, Poetry Wales Press, 1986.

Daniel G. Williams, Ned Thomas and Dai Smith 'The Relevance of Raymond Williams' *Planet: the Welsh Internationalist*, 195, Summer 2009.

4

'A culture where I can breathe'

Stephen Woodhams

In chapter two an attempt was made to understand Raymond Williams against a longer history. What follows may be seen as an attempt to meet that history from the vantage point of how modern Wales has been recovered and understood. Beginning with a common experience from the later 1950s we narrow our focus to review three initiatives that together may be understood as attempts to extend the scope of history to society and culture. One source of encouragement for these progressive historians was the reach toward a 'culture and society' approach inside adult education. From there, attention turns to study of the modern history of Wales in the sixties and the new departures undertaken at the end of that decade, traced here through the South Wales Coalfield History Project, Llafur, the Society for the Study of Welsh Labour History and the South Wales Miners Library.

Adult education had long been a place of experimentation and new departures. It provided a means of learning for those shut out by a small elite university education, too often concerned with keeping its doors guarded against unwanted intrusions. The crossovers of innovative teaching and learning from an external adult education to inside the academy in the post-war decades has been traced elsewhere, but we might note that this moment of change was probably more noticeable in England than in Wales, where the division was always less. What Tom Steele suggests is that the movement of holistic practice into the institution took with it a fluidity for which traditional disciplinary boundaries of internal teaching were less relevant. In a talk entitled 'Adult Education and Social Change', Raymond Williams looked back with some amusement at this moment when he, Richard Hoggart and others moved to internal university teaching, taking with them this more complex form of thinking, and how the authorities, unaware of work done in adult classes, claimed the birth of a new subject. 'Cultural Studies' as it came to be called, took hold across polytechnics and some of the newer universities, challenging the imposed artificial separations into sociology, literature, anthropology, history etc., which can in reality be administrative conveniences, given academic justification by the term 'subjects'.

Yet challenge was not limited to education in a formal sense, rather ways of thinking from adult learning to the new institutions of higher education met with felt responses on the street. Rallies in Trafalgar Square became an image with which the moment has become associated. Events and initiatives followed in rapid succession as the Suez War of 1956 revealed European empire an anachronism, impotent under pressure from an emerging Third World and Cold War relations. Allegation has long been made that the events of Suez were used by the Soviet Union as cover for brutality that crushed the Budapest uprising which, following hard on the heels of revelations from within the Soviet Union, led many to leave western communist parties. If sporadic rallies against seemingly arbitrary events in Suez and Hungary were frustrations, the Easter marches and rallies of the Campaign for Nuclear Disarmament or CND, could seem a positive exertion of long-term effort for reason and humanity.

One specific lead taken in respect of the Hungarian invasion was by a group of historians. Connections between the group and Raymond Williams were discussed in the interviews *Politics and Letters,* published in 1979, where he recalls a school held in 1954 at Netherwood near Hastings to which he was invited as a speaker. The school needs to be placed in the context of developments in adult education and historiography. In the former Williams was to the fore in bringing together literary critics and historians, as had occurred in a course for tutors he convened in Oxford in July 1950. The course, in Williams' view, showed up the seemingly limited thinking of historians in their narrowly defined means of working where hard facts were the only evidential goal.

The school at Netherwood took place in the same period

as the foundation of the Past and Present Society in 1952, the year when it also launched its journal. Perhaps more than any other single organ *Past and Present* took responsibility for addressing alternative approaches to history, with the compass of the journal being: 'social, economic and cultural changes their causes and consequences'. From 1960 came a second inspiration, the Society for the Study of Labour History. In previous decades, Labour History had flourished in adult-education circles and produced significant writers such as Barbara and John Hammond, but the field suffered in the post-war decades as the number of classes declined relative to increases in literary studies. The Society was formed in part to establish a presence for the field within the academy, and among the first persons in the venture, Asa Briggs offered the stature of an establishment figure coupled with the progressive thinking of someone keen to cross boundaries. One stronghold was among Leeds extra-mural teachers with whom Briggs became connected on moving from the Oxford Delegacy in 1955. However, it was at Oxford that he met Raymond Williams, and participated in the 'Literature in Relation to History' course which the latter co-ordinated in 1950. By 1960, Raymond Williams was a respected tutor within the Delegacy. More than this, he gained acknowledgement beyond its circles with his long development of the idea of culture, moving to the complex sociological history that became a feature from *The Long Revolution* onward.

The third initiative ran back to *Our History* and forward to a more unruly child, the History Workshop. *Our History*, though primarily an internal Communist Party publication, made a significant contribution to historical work with its emphasis on local history from below. The Historians Group though known for the generation of eminent figures that came through it, was also a network, with local groups carrying out their own research. Raphael Samuel retained this idea of local groups in cultivating the History Workshop, the early annual gatherings of which witnessed a coming together of people with many interests out of which lively exchanges ensued. The failure was the speed with which the *History Workshop Journal* rejected the egalitarian philosophy of the workshops, to become a very elitist publication that merely recycled arcane theories – increasingly beginning with the word 'post'. Yet the ethos of 'dig where you stand' and 'back to the sources', was inspirational and local history groups have thereby flourished since.

The historical societies, amid new political forms of the fifties and sixties also created an intellectual culture that fed a generation who brought forth a transformed historiography of Wales. The fulcrum for the new work was to be Llafur, and in his 2002 autobiography *Glanmor Williams, A Life* the renowned historian discussed the new generation he helped nurture at Swansea. The ranks included both Hywel Francis and Dai Smith, two prominent names associated with the Coalfield's History Project and the new work that emanated from it in the later sixties. Among others was Merfyn Jones, who came through Sussex University where Asa Briggs, moving from Leeds in 1967, was building up a progressive approach to history. Merfyn Jones would have brought some of that influence, together with that gained at Warwick, with him when he arrived at Swansea in 1971 to join the coalfield's research team.

The broad sweep of historiography in Germany, France and England has been chronicled by, among others, Richard Evans in his *In Defence of History*. The story is one of how in the first two countries, by the mid-twentieth century, the social sciences were already influential in thinking historically. In Germany, the influences of Karl Marx, Max Weber and cultural science associated with names like Wilhelm Dilthey and Ferdinand Tönnies, all served to advance the sense of totality that is perhaps characteristic in Germanic writing. In France, the Annales began as a collective of talents led by the radical historians Lucien Febvre and Marc Bloch. They had been concerned with developing means to carry out more adequate enquiry and explanation of change and continuity over longer periods of time. The citadel they were protesting at was political history. The Annales offered to break from the grip of a history of high politics, using new tools as with Durkheimian insights positing structures such as a 'collective conscious' that by inducing shared beliefs, made society realisable. The Annales offered for investigation layers of history, each subject to its own rhythm of continuance and change, but making these insights ones for historical investigation.

In England, however, history largely remained in the grasp of an empirical political approach. From the fifties, however, influences from across the channel in mainland Europe could begin to be detected. Founding of the Past and Present Society and its journal afforded a vehicle for an Annales perspective in particular, and during the sixties, social history began to be more of a telling presence. In Wales, the turn toward social history was facilitated by the efforts of Glanmor Williams, as much as anyone, after he became Chair of history at Swansea in the mid-1950s. In his autobiography, Glanmor Williams records how he was asked

to draft a paper on what might be done in the field of recent Welsh history, so I outlined a scheme for the study of Welsh society and politics between *c.*1846 and 1950. It seemed to me for some time that this area was being ignored and serious examination was long overdue.

To appreciate the scope of this proposed field of study we need to remember something of the history of Welsh society, discussed in chapter two. The rapidity of industrialisation had meant that iron, coal and steel towns had grown perhaps too fast to allow for effective control by a progressive middle class. A consequence of this was a preponderantly working-class society which became, by 1920, politically as well as socially the defining factor in local communities. It was arguably this that helped shape the second and third generations of academics in Welsh institutions, growing up as they did in the years between 1914 and the fifties.

The wider historical picture then helps in our understanding of those who followed the template for historiography set out by Glanmor Williams. In his Inaugural Lecture in 1959, his plea for the study of modern history stressed two features; first, a deliberate emphasis on social history, and second, moving the point at which the modern history of Wales should be dated. Previously, the emphasis in Welsh history had been pre-modern, indeed a great deal of it moved no further than the 1536 Act of Union with England when so-called modern history was deemed to begin. Glanmor Williams moves the break point forward to around 1760, arguing that for a large part of the Welsh population it was the industrial revolution that really figured as the period when a modern society could meaningfully be understood to be experienced. To argue for such a recasting of history displays his profound understanding of various periods and this is amply demonstrated in a late collection of essays published in 1979 as *Religion, Language and Nationality*. However, it was not only the periodisation of Welsh history that Glanmor Williams was challenging. Traditionalists had taken the Victorian concern with the nation-state as the prism through which to view Wales. By contrast, Glanmor Williams argued that Wales was better understood if studied as a social history.

At the risk of overbrief simplicity, the contrast might be set out thus. England is perhaps an ideal type for the application of a political and constitutional history, with the sixteenth-century Tudor Reformation offering itself as prime reference point. Wales, by contrast, had a less obvious existence as a political nation, its unity, even before 1282, being less than secure. Studied as social history, however,

Wales, its people and their experience made for a different kind of coherent explication, as chapter two sought to demonstrate.

Glanmor Williams' inaugural lecture would have been heard by his adult student and friend, Ieuan Gwynedd Jones, one of the earliest yields of the initiatives undertaken at Swansea. Later Ieuan Gwynedd Jones would sum up the approach to Welsh history in a phrase, 'As a social historian – and the historian of Wales can be no other...' Later still, the point was reiterated by another Swansea-educated historian Neil Evans, in a review of the historiography of Wales and the Welsh for the journal *Social History*. Elsewhere Neil Evans traced a longer historiography, from the Victorians through to the seventies. The earlier concern with state formation and the actions of nation-states may be seen as distinctive of Victorian historiography, in contrast, the seventies were marked by the turn to a social and cultural history which placed people at its centre. Wales was well-placed to take advantage of the shift in perception.

Gauged by literary and poetic work, industrial working-class Wales had been viewed as something of a downward slide from the culture of nineteenth-century liberal rural Wales. The view rested upon a number of assumptions. For some the key feature was language – there was a Cymru, where Cymraeg was the first language and defined the population as Cymreig. Poetry and prose were then assumed as the fullest expression of the language and were rated higher than anything that might be produced by an anglicised hand. Industrial working-class South Wales therefore self-excluded itself from this purer Cymru, because of a shift, magnified in the first half of the twentieth century, toward English as the first language. For others the fault lay in industrialisation itself, which seemed a decline in a way of life as compared with that of an idealised rural Gwerin or folk. The view was perhaps typical of romantic nostalgia, where a pre-industrial world served as vessel for an organic culture in which people lived closer with nature and kept to a simpler, purer life. Not unrelated was the religious version, where increasing secularisation led to weaker moral standards than had been lived in a Cymru of chapel observing people, and for whom the Word provided sure judgement by which to live. Alternatively, the perception might be that anglicised industrial workers were the by-product of a colonial invasion that threatened the existence of Cymru. If couched in the language of moral cultural, these condemnatory views could be augmented by a political strand in which a left-leaning movement, of miners in particular, was a descent into socialism that could be defined as ungodly, alien and poisonous. Separately, and together, these grounds meant that any written expression from industrial South Wales could only be corrupted when compared with the finer poetry and prose of nineteenth-century Cymru – be that rural, liberal or religious. In such antagonistic circumstance, the 'Welsh industrial novel' must be seen as a significant literary output from the interwar years onward. What the work of Lewis Jones, Jack Jones, and of course Gwyn Thomas, taught, was the paucity of recorded experience of industrialisation in Wales. It was this lack which Glanmor Williams addressed in his call for greater resources devoted to the study of modern Wales, as defined by the rupture of the industrial revolution. In turn, it was first to the filling of that void in the history of Wales, and second to alter the priorities by which that past was assembled, that the efforts emanating from Swansea, were directed.

Glanmor Williams and Ieuan Gwynedd Jones were coincidentally born in 1920 and Gwyn Alf Williams 1925, so that each of them had direct experience of the desperate economic and social devastation that dealt the coalfield from the 1920s on. Their entry into university life was, like that of Raymond Williams (born 1921), around the time of the Second World War, and during the immense changes brought about by the 1945 Labour Government. Their life experience then encompassed the tragedy of economic dislocation, but also drew on the response of common action made in community and neighbourly ties through workplace, chapel and union. War reinforced both the sense of tragedy and of common sharing but also created an aspiration of building a new and different future. The real gains to people's lives in health, housing and education after 1945 confirmed the sense of collective effort learnt in childhood and youth.

In 1954, Ieuan Gwynedd Jones was encouraged at Swansea by Glanmor Williams to begin the work later identified in the latter's 1959 inaugural lecture. Jones rapidly established his position at Swansea, contributing to research and teaching and beyond that to local history societies. A bibliography of his work up to 1987 offers an interesting insight into his generation and background, with many articles appearing not in the semi-official organs of academic history, but as local publications written for readerships connected with a particular place and always inclusive in their accessibility. Ieuan Gwynedd Jones went on to become Professor of History at Aberystwyth, affording support for the start of Llafur, and playing a significant part in establishing the modern history of Wales. It is difficult to generalise too far, but we are dealing with a question of generations, the experience of moving from working-class environments, and on to an expansion of higher education which pulled in people who in other contexts might have worked in adult education or related fields. In Wales this process, then, occurred differently from England for reasons discussed in chapter two, and it meant that the transition from manual labouring to university teaching might take two generations or less.

This then was the background against which the project to recover the history of the South Wales Coalfield was conceived by Hywel Francis and Dai Smith as PhD students together at Swansea from 1968 and subsequently developed under the auspices of Glanmor Williams. In brief, a group was pulled together at Swansea, supported through a Social Science Research Council award in 1971 for an initial year. Their aim was to recover a record of the coalfield which otherwise was becoming fragmented, with much lost through inevitable natural and human wear and tear. The group, led by Merfyn Jones, consisted of a small number of prime researchers, whose industry Glanmor Williams highlighted in his autobiography. The aims of the project were to find and retrieve lodge records, minutes, accounts, letters and memorabilia from the miners' halls and institutes, and where possible, some of the collections from the libraries. The holdings of libraries varied widely as did the number of miners contributing to a particular Welfare Hall. In all, there were over a hundred miners' institutes and libraries with examples of the largest in the Rhondda where some, such as Clydach Vale, held over 15,000 volumes.

The Research Council supported project was expanded to include oral history and was completed between 1971 and 1974, but the essential work continued. Dai Smith joined the history Department in 1971 and Hywel Francis complemented the Project team. Institutionally, perhaps the major outcome has been the remarkable South Wales Miners Library. Established in October 1973, the Miners' Library was the inheritor of the past generations of miners' libraries and institutes. Hywel Francis joined the Extra-Mural Department at Swansea and became the Tutor Librarian of the Miners' Library as it functioned as a centre for both Research and Adult Education. One major published outcome of the Coalfield History Project was *The Fed: A History of the South Wales Miners in the Twentieth Century*. First published in 1980, the book received support from the South Wales Region of the National Union of Mineworkers, but its subject matter held an appeal far beyond the coalfield. Written by Hywel Francis and Dai Smith the book keeps to the history of the Union but places it in the context of the coalfield and the society people made for themselves. Links to the research work of the Coalfield History Project are clear, with notes containing numerous references to recorded interviews, while the photo-plates included several housed in the archive. A new edition of *The Fed*, with a Centenary Foreword appeared in 1998.

Alongside the Coalfield History Project came the inspiration for Llafur, the Society for the Study of Welsh Labour History. Founded in Swansea by a small group of historians in 1970, it rapidly became the focal point for wider Welsh involvement. The full commencement of Llafur as an organisation in 1971 included a symposium at which spoke substantial figures connected with Welsh labour history. Months later Gwyn Alf Williams was to give the Society's first lecture. From the fifties, his own town of Merthyr and the events surrounding the popular uprising of 1831 had been a spine to his thinking, and this was his topic at the inaugural meeting. The lecture appeared as the first article of the journal's first number, signifying to a wider readership perhaps that Llafur was to be a forum for sharing histories, underpinned by intellectual credibility.

The success of the Llafur Society was immediate and apparent in the growth in numbers. Deian Hopkins, in his account of the formation of Llafur, records that, 'From thirty-eight in its first year, the Society membership increased to 450 in two years.' Even allowing for block membership of 200 underwritten by the National Union of Mineworkers, the increase was remarkable. An indication of the Society's popularity was at an event in 1973 to mark the seventy-fifth anniversary of the South Wales Miners' Federation; 350 attended to hear Michael Foot talk on his forthcoming biography of Aneurin Bevan. An early achievement was to bring together people to share their many experiences of coal, metals or similar work in Wales. Commencement of the journal, the first issue of which appeared in 1972, offered a means of reaching a much wider audience and eliciting contributions and support. Early issues of Llafur contained articles on the coalfield and significant moments of conflict, notably the 1926 General Strike, remembered in the issue for 1976. Yet writers also looked beyond these high points to explore religious practice, health, culture and sport, in order to offer a rounded picture of industrial Wales. Absent in that account, however, was rural Wales, the poverty left behind and worsened by the loss of the most economically active part of a population. Beyond that, rural Wales was missing for its contribution to the making of modern Wales, in not only people but also the necessary food stuff and other raw materials for the urbanised life of the steel and coal towns. Raymond Williams would pick up on these interconnections at different points; critically in *The Country and the City*, where familial and economic relations could be found to have a longer history and where lines of produce and money might flow parallel with migration and new settlement.

Interconnections can be found too in imaginative form as in *Border Country*, the rail line running southwest to the coalfield and east to the midlands of England, and then Morgan's initiative to collect and deliver food stuffs from around Pandy to the striking miners. Again, in *Second*

Generation, where the car-works' dependent families in Oxford are pulled back to their connections across the border, as in Peter's running away from the scene of his parent's conflict. Then in *The Fight for Manod* we again meet Matthew, now caught between the formal investigation he is commissioned to complete for authorities back in London, and the obvious needs of local people which were being overridden by economic and political powers both state and commercial. Written during the oil crisis of 1973–74 *Manod* is perhaps the place where Williams might have best imagined connections of country and city, if the novel had been of adequate length to describe the new technologies cited for the proposed experiment in forms of living.

An appropriately personal note begins an address entitled 'The Social Significance of 1926' given to a joint Llafur and National Union of Mineworkers commemorative conference marking the strike's fiftieth anniversary. Raymond starts not with an historical outline of the strike and lockout but his own journey that day:

> I came down this morning from a village above Aberga-venny: travelling the quite short distance to this centre of the mining valleys, and travelling also, in memories, the connections and the distance between one kind of country and another. In 1926, in that village, my father was one of three signalmen in the old Great Western Railway box...

> Consider first that specific situation. These men at that country station were industrial workers, trade unionists, in a

small group within a primarily rural and agricultural economy. All of them like my father, still had close connections with that agricultural life... At the same time, by the very fact of the railway, with trains passing through, from the cities, from the factories, from the ports from the collieries, ... they were part of a modern industrial working class.

Acknowledgement of these memories is fitting. Elsewhere Williams has referred to his having from the mid-1950s to relearn the history of Wales. The timing may be significant since, working on *Border Country* in those years, he talked over events that contributed to the chapter on the General Strike with his father. There is here a question of Williams' life which is, as yet, not clear, since to relearn in the mid-fifties a history appropriate to his father's account of 1926 would have meant reading against the grain of much existing work, where the tendency was to look to the tradition of a national, political framework. Yet by drawing on scattered comments we can identify at least one suggestive influence though it is likely not to have been the only source. In writing *Border Country* we know Williams was responding to problems in the Welsh novel. Of course Dylan Thomas' verbal excess created difficulties that needed to be avoided. However, there were others who offered accounts deeply marked by an experience of South Wales and 1926. Williams has spoken of being 'aware of the Welsh writers about the working class of the interwar period'; Lewis Jones' *Cwmardy* and *We Live* being among the most likely volumes Williams read. It is of course not the whole story and at least Aberystwyth's David Williams, earlier inspirer of Welsh historiography, may have been a figure of who Williams was aware. It is, however, conceivable that when Williams speaks of having in the 1950s to learn the history of Wales, in place of the social history then largely unwritten, it was those historian writers of fiction that were for him the most immediate references.

By 1976, Raymond had developed an explicit holding together in his mind of country and city. Yet to present the connection so directly to a new generation of more industrial-minded historians with their roots in the coalfield was still, perhaps a brave step. For many of the young of the seventies there was too easy an assumption that the urban was the site of progressive action, the rural a bastion of conservatism. In the context of Wales, that picture could take the form of landlord, Anglican clergy, dissenting zealot and quiescent agricultural labourer. Yet that picture would be a distortion, hiding conflicts as between Anglican landlord and dissenting worker, their struggle over the use of land and the dispossession of its population. Wales was a place where country and city co-existed closely and where economy and culture were reproduced through a way of life.

A collection of essays commissioned and edited by Dai Smith and published in 1980 as *A People and a Proletariat*, was, as its introduction suggests, a further challenge, indeed a deliberate provocation:

> ... we cannot be confident about the social history of modern Wales since, at each and every point that seems

to matter..., the simplistic view should be, and now is, open to challenge. A few bold conquistadores of the historical profession over the last quarter century, from David Williams to Kenneth O. Morgan, have carved out and lucidly structured imposing narratives of the recent history of Wales. That was the first step out of the dark. The editors and contributors to this book would like to think, ... that this collection will encourage the taking of the next step.

The content of the book covered a range of subjects but with the stress on industrial Wales from the mid-nineteenth century on. However, in Raymond Williams' review, it is two offerings that stand apart from this emphasis that receive particular attention:

> This is industrial South Wales recovering its actual history, beyond the simplifying images, but there may be just as much effect in, for example, the essay by Merfyn Jones on 'Class and society in 19th Century Gwynedd', in which the image of a backward but proud, organic and unified culture dissolves, or in David Jenkins's 'Rural Society Inside Outside', which in its fine evidence of language and practice explores what was and was not a 'natural community' and an 'organic folk'.

The solicited review appeared in the fortnightly magazine *Arcade*, for which Dai Smith served as Literary Editor, at the end of 1980. It is reprinted in Daniel Williams' edited collection *Who Speaks for Wales?* and provides a point from which to explore links between the development of a social history of Wales and Raymond Williams' own evolving thinking of Wales in terms of nation and nationalism. Published in 1971, the first essay in the collection is 'Who Speaks For Wales?' being a review of Ned Thomas' *The Welsh Extremist*. The date's significance is that it follows shortly on from when Raymond Williams suggests his greater contact with thinkers in Wales commenced. Ned Thomas too had had to work through his relation to a people and a country, and the book was an extension of that process. More than an individual referent point, *The Welsh Extremist* followed on the heels of a genuine widespread campaign to assert the rights of people, nation and language. For the campaigns of civil disobedience, Thomas felt a ready assent, placing himself as one of the 'followers' who wanted the direct action to succeed. True, Thomas is uneasy about the acceptance by a minority of violence in their tactics, but he is sympathetic to the reasons behind this so-called 'extremism'. *The Welsh Extremist* comes from a different place than say *Llafur*, or *A People and a Proletariat*. The latter pair focused first on an industrial working class and, in South Wales, principally this meant English speakers. *The Welsh Extremist* sought in part to reach across the divisions with which Ned Thomas, as himself a returning migrant, was needing to come to terms with. The book addresses a fractured present informed by a fragmented past, and its discussion ranges over 'the language issue', whether there was one Wales, two, or even three, the place of political parties and Plaid Cymru's function as a nationalist focus. Ned Thomas contended that an elected assembly should exist and that it should represent the broadest opinion possible in Wales. With this and more Raymond Williams at the time concurred, going on to locate our 'extremist's' cause in other progressive movements,

> Black power in the United States, civil rights in Ulster, the language in Wales, are experiences comparable in this respect to the student movement and to women's liberation.

The comparisons demonstrate his growing sense of the complexity of what was a new situation. Through his review of *The Welsh Extremist*, and from a talk entitled 'Are We Becoming More Divided?' prepared a few years later for Granada Television, we can appreciate Raymond Williams' recognition of problems posed by tensions between populations and regions, and the histories in Wales that produced them. Something of this awareness may be recognised in two examples. In the first, Raymond Williams answers a question about his relationship to Wales, in the second, the question is answered by Matthew Price:

> Yes, a big change started to happen from the late sixties. There was a continuity in a quite overwhelming feeling about the land of Wales; as feeling and writing that stays through. But then I began to have more contacts... and I found this curious effect. Suddenly England, bourgeois

England, wasn't my point of reference anymore. I was a
Welsh European, and at both levels felt different.

Tom Meurig smiled, looking across at Peter as if
resuming a discussion.

'Yes,' he said, noticing Matthew's interception of the
look, 'we've been arguing about you.'

'Why not?' Matthew said.

'But don't get it the wrong way round. Peter was
defending you. It was I who was asking what you meant
by coming here.'

'With what possibilities?'

Meurig laughed.

'Well, Matthew Price,' he said smiling, 'you're an exile.
Perhaps, I don't know, a voluntary exile. So that none of
us yet knows your commitment to Wales.'

Matthew leaned forward.

'Enough of a commitment to know the divisions,' he
said, sharply.

When, then, Raymond Williams' wrote reviews of the
new history of Wales, it was part of a coming together of
paths. Growing up, Welsh Wales and England had both
seemed at variance to his border experience. Yet the late
sixties and into the seventies were a different time and
context to the thirties. Different too from when, away
in south-east England, Raymond had worked through
drafts of *Border Country*. The change was the quest for an
intellectually more complex history, adequate for a modern

Wales. Attempts to delineate a 'Wales' by means of political unity, in the manner of Victorian English historiography, were of limited reach. A 'Union' from the 1530s was hardly a date to which people could readily relate any more than that of 1282. Glanmor Williams called for the moving forward of the dividing line marking the start of modern Wales to around 1760. More than that, he had called for fifty per cent of scholarly resources to be put to the exploration of the period after that date. Here focus has been on the coalfield project and Llafur, elsewhere Neil Evans has cited how histories shifted their weight of pages so that a greater proportion of a book was given to the modern period as defined in the Glanmor Williams 1959 lecture. Likewise, in the series of monographs offered by the Board of Celtic Studies the great majority now address modern history. When, however, Raymond Williams recalls in *Politics and Letters* that, after his childhood experience, he had had to learn Welsh history again in the later 1950s, he was typically ahead of others. The moment referred to by him coincided with writing that eventually became *Border Country*, and when a call for modern history was still something uttered by lone voices. As such Williams had to read from the margins since that alternative historical record did not yet exist. This must have been difficult, reading back against a history only a tip of which had informed his schooling. That Williams recognised in the eventual new history a common ground, may then have been cause for relief after his earlier struggles to make sense of Wales out of historical writing that, as in his childhood, simply did not meet with his lived experience.

Raymond Williams

Border Country, 1960, Library of Wales, Parthian, 2006.

'The Social Significance of 1926', Llafur, 2, 2 1977, reprinted in *Who Speaks for Wales?*, 2003.

The Fight for Manod, 1979, Hogarth, 1988.

The Welsh Industrial Novel, 1979, reprinted in *Who Speaks for Wales?*, 2003.

Politics and Letters, 1979, Verso, 2015.

Read All About Us: Raymond Williams, BBC Wales tx 21/10/96.

Who Speaks for Wales? Raymond Williams, edited Daniel Williams, UWP, 2003.

Other works

Neil Evans, 'Writing the social history of modern Wales: approaches, achievements and problems', *Social History* vol.17, no. 3, October 1992.

Hywel Francis and Dai Smith, *The Fed, A History of the South Wales Miners*, UWP, 1998.

Hywel Francis and Sian Williams, *Do Miners Read Dickens?*, Parthian, 2013.

Deian Hopkins, 'Llafur: Labour History Society and People's Remembrancer 1970–2009', in John McIlroy et al eds, *Making History*, Maney, 2010.

Geraint Jenkins, *The People's Historian Professor Gwyn Williams (1925–1995)*, Aberystwyth, 1996.

Llafur, The Society for the Study of Welsh Labour History, *Llafur*, Vols. 1&2, 1972–1979.

Dai Smith, *Raymond Williams: A Warrior's Tale*, Parthian, 2008.

Dai Smith, *In the Frame: Memory in Society 1910–2010*, Parthian, 2010.

Tom Steele, *The Emergence of Cultural Studies*, Lawrence and Wishart, 1997.

Colin Thomas, *The People's Remembrancer*, (BBC Wales/ S4C) Teliesyn, 1995.

Gwyn Thomas, *The Dark Philosophers*, Library of Wales, Parthian, 2006.

Gwyn Thomas, *The Alone to the Alone,* Library of Wales, Parthian, 2008.

Glanmor Williams, *Glanmor Williams A Life*, UWP, 2002.

The South Wales Coalfield History Project, Report 1971–1974, Social Science Research Council.

5

Dream of a Country

Elizabeth Allen

In the early pages of Raymond Williams' third novel, *The Fight for Manod*, an adult Matthew Price stands on the mountainside above a mid-Wales valley, looking at the country before him, remembering

> the boy on the mountain, looking down at Glynmawr, seeing the history of his country in the shapes of the land. He saw the meeting of the valleys, and England blue in the distance. On the high ground to the east were the Norman castles, and the disputed land in their shadow. On the limestone scarp to the south was the line of the ironmaster, the different frontier: on the near side the valleys still green and wooded, on the far side blackened with collieries and slagheaps and grey huddled terraces. The history had been clear at the moment of going away.

The account of the landscape captures themes running
through Williams at the time of writing *The Fight for Manod*
(henceforth *Manod*), begun in 1965, though not completed
until 1978. We appreciate this the more if the novel is placed
alongside the historical and critical work *The Country and
the City*, which Williams began writing in the same year.
Both books are centrally concerned with both how land is
owned and how it is imagined. In *The Country and the City*,
Williams demonstrates how the ownership of land and the
social relations that have followed are taken for granted in
English literature. Reaching back over centuries, Williams
illustrates that historical and contrived relations of land and
work came to be assumed as natural and given.

The relation between the two texts is an interesting
one. In *Politics and Letters*, he tells his interviewers that 'by
the late sixties' he perceived the 'whole country and city
relation… as for me the crucial relation in contemporary
social analysis.' 'Much of the wider project of the novel',
he says, 'had gone into' a recast version of *The Country and
the City*, leaving *Manod* as 'an alternative shape.' Yet it is in
this more restricted, fictional shape that we find tensions
in meanings and relations of country and city, local and
national, past and present, come together in the dreams
and anxieties of a possible future.

As the title suggests, the action of the novel centres on
struggles for control of a place and its future. The fight for
Manod is perceived as multi-dimensional. At the most
accessible level of plot, it is the fight for ownership of fields
and buildings which may if altered from their present use

be made to create profit. It is a fight for ownership and for control which, as Williams comments in the final chapter of *The Country and the City*, is not confined to depopulated rural areas, but is part of 'the international system as a whole.' Referring to a dispute then raging over the development and beneficiaries of an area of central London he writes,

> It then does not surprise me that the complaints in Covent Garden echo the complaints of the commoners, since the forces of improvement and development – an amalgam of financial and political power which is pursuing different ends from those of any local community but which has its own and specific internal rationale – are in a fundamental sense similar, as phases of capitalist enterprise.

The future of Manod is inevitably to be decided by priorities other than those set by local needs and desires. But it is, too, a dispute over control of the representation of the place, how it is talked of and understood and thus defined and controlled. This, the third of the Welsh trilogy, brings together Matthew Price from *Border Country* and Peter Owen of *Second Generation*, now employed as consultants for a proposed new city that will take the name of Manod from one of the mid-Wales villages and towns which it will subsume. Having moved into a local cottage, Matthew's understanding of the place and the project based on mountains of official reports is supplemented by his day-to-day experience of the economic tensions of this depopulated region as demonstrated in the lives of the neighbours, farmers and agricultural workers, whose family relations are brought under continuous pressure by the need to make a living from this marginal land. Matthew and Peter, with some guidance from the Plaid Cymru politician Tom Meurig, learn of a conspiracy to make massive profits tied to the proposed development. This plot has a local agent, builder and entrepreneur John Dance, but behind him are national and international pressures. Although the plot is uncovered, the fate of this dying rural community is kept unresolved, Williams thereby preventing closure in the narrative.

Is resolution possible when even the name Manod is a disputed territory? In the novel's first chapter Matthew Price has a meeting with Robert Lane, who featured in *Second Generation*, the second novel of the Welsh trilogy, as a lecturer at Oxford, but who is now based at the Department of the Environment as an adviser to the Labour government. In an initial discussion with Lane, Matthew responds simply to the first reference to Manod that 'it's about forty miles from where I grew up.' But, says Robert Lane, 'up here, it's not primarily a place. It's a name, a code sign, perhaps even a symbol.' The existence of these two dimensions of abstraction and experience, their apparent hostility as values and the necessity of their co-existence, is of central interest in this novel. Lane, in his role as government official, understands Manod only as a sign and this erasure of the people, the material place and the work which goes to produce it, the 'hills and fields soaked with labour' to which he refers in the essay 'Welsh Culture', cannot be acceptable.

The very form and detail of the novel construct for us not an empty space to be written on from above but a land of already existing sites of community and working relations. For those making a living here, Manod is not a symbol but a materiality expressed in a discourse of highly specific knowledge of the land itself and of lived relations. When the farmer Gethin Jenkins works to rescue his young neighbour Ivor Vaughan, who is trapped under a tractor, 'the angle at which the holding rope would run was exactly related to the complicated slope and to the way the tractor was lying. It was as if he could feel every inch of the ground.' So it is that near the end of the novel Matthew is still contending with the official dehumanising discourse which uses Manod as shorthand for the project and thereby ignores 'the actual place'. But, of course, the ground that Gethin feels exists not only in its physical weight but as another disputed piece of territory in terms of the complexities of ownership and inheritance which structure the story. It is not just a place on a map, but a place in history.

The account of the changes in ownership of the location of the tractor accident, the Pentre farm now owned by the Vaughan family, is, in content and in tone, another nailing of the myth which *The Country and the City* destroys: the conflation of the English country house and the English country estate with a 'natural' order and an essence of England. Until 1948 the Vaughan family have farmed Pentre as tenants of the Mortimers but were able to buy the land when the estate 'was broken up and sold to meet death duties.' A London magazine is quoted as mourning this loss of a traditional estate, 'an ancient and honourable tradition of landowning has ended in the brutal materialism of post-war England intent on destroying its own past.' The Vaughans keep the article but do not share its sense of loss. 'An ancient and honourable tradition of landowning, Thomas Vaughan told his children, was now just beginning: now in 1948 when Pentre was owned by the family that for a hundred and ten years had been working it.' They are seen as acting out the fight back against the distortion of history and erasure of working people from the countryside with which *The Country and the City* so memorably engages.

Seeing 'the history of this country in the shapes of the land', but also through his acquired knowledge of patterns of migration in the wider socio-economic system, Matthew's educated consciousness is forced to perceive Manod through multiple lenses. The solicitor Bryn Walters in his first interview with Matthew gives clear privilege to 'experience', stating briskly that, seeing social method 'in the raw', he has little time for mere reading. But, while in contention with Lane, Matthew defends 'experience', here he contends that abstraction has its necessary place, 'The rawer the practice, the more need for theory.' In Williams' essay on the 1926 General Strike, he writes of workers, 'Urged to act in solidarity… not by place or work or physical connection, but in essence by an idea, an idea that may even contradict their immediate local and material interest: the idea of the class, the solidarity of the class.'

The problem of relating to different perspectives is made explicit in the form adopted in the second chapter of *Manod*. Here contrasting perspectives are represented through different modes of discourse: the chapter is divided into seven sections discontinuous not only in time but in style. In the first, when Matthew is looking at the country through his window at night, the language is designed as appropriate for the intensity of his responses, 'A strange waitingness, as if it was not yet known what would come out of the shadows.' After this heightened response of someone interacting with, rather than simply observing, landscape, we have a flat, textbook style account of the typography: 'Manod stands on a plain... to the west... rise the successive long whaleback ridges...' These distinct and irreconcilable methods of representing the same place demonstrate what Matthew comes to see as the problem for Manod: those interested in the plans for the new city have different ways of seeing that cannot be held together to form a coherent picture. When, having made his official report on the findings on the insider dealings, Matthew and his wife Susan drive away, 'the long valley lay below them, the river silver under the sun. From the height, it seemed quiet and empty. It was difficult to imagine the lodged papers that now effectively determined it. It was too great a disparity for any single perspective.'

Throughout the novel, Matthew's fight is an attempt to bring those various perspectives, which can be summarised as the tensions between experience and abstraction, into relation. Much of the important critical work on Williams has addressed this same tension. Terry Eagleton understands the tension as existing between two senses of culture on two sides of a border. On one side lies 'the lived particularities of place, region, nature, the body' and on the other 'educated consciousness.' Williams, he believes, understood that 'the social reality lay in the *tension*, not either pole taken in isolation.' In an essay which focuses on Williams' fiction, David Harvey clarifies the wider political context of the tension. He discusses his experience of the proposed closure of the Rover car plant in Cowley, Oxford, interestingly the same plant which features centrally in *Second Generation*. The defining need, he writes, is to agree on which parameters of *space* are relevant. What is the community here? Is it the workplace only or the Cowley community outside the workplace? Should the discussion extend to encompass Britain, or indeed Europe, with its 'incredible overcapacity of the automobile industry'? One cannot, Harvey argues, hold that

> what is right and good for the militant shop stewards of Cowley can simply be extended to the wider society. Other levels and kinds of abstraction have to be deployed if socialism is to break out of its local bonds and become a viable alternative to capitalism as a working mode of production and social relations.

The relevance of this to the debates on Manod is clear. Like the Cowley shop stewards, the lives of the inhabitants of Manod operate with what Williams identified as 'a militant particularism'. This, however, needs to be understood as one term in the dialectic, the other being 'the struggle to

achieve sufficient critical distance and detachment.' Harvey
acknowledges the difficulties that Williams experiences in
holding the terms in proper tension but asserts the absolute
value of maintaining this pressure in terms of practical
political action. 'The core task' writes Harvey, is 'the return
of theory to the world of daily practical politics.' *Manod*
is a novel where the difficulty of the move from the micro
to the macro perspectives of land, from the material to the
imaginary, is foregrounded in both form and content, and
where the political implications of this move are insisted
upon. The fight for Manod can be read as a fight for an
appropriate representation of the place.

At the more traditional political level, the relation of the
proposed city to historical policy decisions – or the absence
of them – on the future of rural Wales is an interesting one.
It was in 1965, the year in which Williams began the novel,
that the first Secretary of State for Wales, James Griffiths,
proposed a new town for rural mid-Wales. In an interesting
move between history and fiction, the historian Kenneth
Morgan comments that the concept of a 'new community
of 60,000 people somewhere in the nearly deserted Severn
Valley close to Caersws in Montgomeryshire (was) turned
down in 1967' and 'did not re-emerge' until nearer the
publication of *Manod* in 1979. 'As report followed report
and debate followed debate, the problems of rural Wales
remained as intractable as ever.' While Williams' creative
version of this story of frustration gives due weight to
those repeated reports and debates, it also offers a vital new
element. There was already a New Town in Wales, not much

more than twenty miles from Williams' Pandy. Cwmbran, the New Town designed to provide employment opportunities in the south-east of Wales, had been established in 1949, developing around a number of existing villages in the Eastern Valley of Monmouthshire and laying no claims to aesthetic or technological innovation. Manod is to be something different, a city of the future.

The 'intractable problem', as Morgan calls it, is partially generated by the suffocating weight of paper, procedures and power which construct project 'Manod'. As the government adviser Robert Lane warns Matthew at their first interview, 'The political papers are twenty feet thick.' 'Like most other new worlds', it is, he says, 'just a debris of yellowing paper.' Is the Ministry where these heaps of paper are housed, then, a mid-twentieth century Circumlocution Office from which no outcome can ever be possible? The austere façade in the 'street of the Ministries' conceals the real place of power, a 'glittering, dazzling' glass tower which, as in a fairy story, may only be reached by crossing a bridge. The very fabric of the building works to frustrate. The arrangement of the room where a crucial meeting is held leaves Matthew desperately jostled and, when he complains of being unable to hear vital new information, the Minister responds blandly, 'This has always been a difficult room.' The explicit politics of the proposal are far from simple. Even without the revelations of the machinations of Anglo–Belgian Community Developments, the concept is clearly one whose advocates have different motives and agendas. A possible motive, as suggested by Tom Meurig, is to settle an English colony in a Welsh valley. Alternatively, as Matthew argues, the potential benefit is a more general repopulation of a declining area – one where the local newspaper records no births or marriages but only deaths. A third possibility, described by Lane, is a dual benefit, moving jobs to a rural area, where unemployment is chronically high and moving people from 'great sprawling and jammed conurbations' where 'life is simply breaking down' to a 'better environment'. In the fight for Manod the motives of the supporters of the project, even those openly articulated, may not be compatible.

These arguments are those which might be posed for any scheme of intensive or extensive urban development in rural areas. It is the specifics of the Manod project which mark it as radically different in its social implications. For Manod will be a city made in the present for the future, 'There is not a city like this anywhere', says Robert Lane. If it were to be built,

> it will be one of the first human settlements, anywhere in the world, to have been conceived, from the beginning, in post-industrial terms and with a post-industrial tech-nology… a working city, an advanced working city in that kind of country. With the river, the mountains, it would be a marvellous place.

Its spatial configuration is enticing, it is not intended to build on all the agricultural land, but to develop centres, 'set back on the higher ground, hill-towns really… Between each… at least four or five miles of quite open country which would go on being farmed.' In this Tuscan-style vision, one may read echoes of the D. H. Lawrence's ideal of which Williams was concurrently writing in *The Country and the City*. Lawrence rages against 'the false town' but is certainly not hostile to 'the Italian cities on which he often draws for examples.' His complaint is that 'the English character has failed to develop the real *urban* side of a man, the civic side.' This plan for Manod is indeed a city as an object of desire, and, in terms of technology, not an impossible dream. For in 1973, in the middle of the years during which *Manod* was written, Williams visited the United States of America and worked in California, at the Department of Communications in Stanford. Here he experienced the new technology of video cassettes, satellite transmission, large-screen receivers and cable distribution. The outcome of this visit was the 1974 publication *Television: Technology and Cultural Form*. Williams had seen the future but was unsure how, in social terms, it would work. *Television* concludes with the argument that this new technology offers such 'extreme social choices'. One is that this vast new 'communication and information-sharing' potential may be used to further 'the long revolution towards an educated and participatory democracy', which is at the heart of Williams' vision. Or, under the guise of 'choice and competition a few para-national corporations… could reach further into our lives, at every level from news to psychodrama, until individual response to any different kinds of experience and problem become almost limited to choice among the programmed possibilities.'

The frightening prescience of the nightmare scenario sticks in the mind, but it is not in 1974, offered as an inevitable future. The necessity, says Williams in the last lines of *Television*, is for 'decisions to be taken now'. For actions to be taken 'its first conditions are information, analysis, education, discussion.' The book is offered as 'contribution' and 'incentive' to this debate and *Manod* can in part be read as another contribution. The novel uncovers dubious practice at local, national and international level, and Peter Owen, never a character to take a nuanced position, storms off to write an exposé in newspaper and book form. Yet Matthew persists in his belief in the possibility that the project offers 'a unique opportunity... to explore new social patterns, new social relations.' It is not the glamour of technology which matters but precisely the potential for a huge step forward in the Long Revolution.

It is perhaps a weakness of the novel that questions of how the new technology and social patterns might be configured are left at the margin. This may be explained by the demands of publishers for what Williams considered to be brevity, and in *Politics and Letters* he remarks that when he had drafted 'six out of a projected thirty chapters, moving at the only pace at which I judged it could be properly done', the estimated length would have been 'well over two hundred thousand words.' The issue of length persists in the interview, and Williams concludes, 'that it's not, of course, for better or worse, the novel I originally set out to write.' Perhaps had he insisted on something longer than the final novel, essential themes might have been developed.

There was also the perceived problem of 'projecting and imagining a future, but, deliberately, not as futurism but as a future that has in some way to come through from a rooted present.' This would help to explain why there is no exploration of the new social attitudes which could be established through new modes of communication in a city whose spatial design, with its hill-towns and open country between, manages to combine the visual charm of Tuscany and cutting-edge technology. But even this tantalising outline serves to make the point that those critics who read Williams as mired in some sentimental version of a Welsh past or pastoral idyll are failing to pay attention to central elements in his writing. The relationship of past and present is understood as fraught, but the focus is on the future.

There are two conversations with Beth, a central character from the 'second generation', and in these Matthew is at his most open and visionary. The problematic relationship of the past and the possible future informs their talk, and Williams in these provides for Matthew a means for him to express his desires, which Beth sets off with her concrete balance. In contrast, in discussions with officialdom, Matthew quite properly maintains the materiality of Manod, a place and people not reducible to a codeword or a symbol. The novel's intensity of detail, its insistence on the country as produced by labour, constantly generates the same emphasis. However, with Beth the emphasis shifts, there is the acknowledgement, the celebration, of the 'pure idea'. It is vital for survival. Such an idea, he tells Beth, belongs specifically 'to this country'. It is 'a pure passion for a different world.' When Beth inquires whether he understands this pure passion as motivating the existing population of the valley, he insists on the abstract nature of the idea, 'In what has moved through them. In their religion, in their politics. It's not ever been cynical, not ever resigned. It's been a dream if you like, but a dream of a country.' The embodiment of this dream, he goes on, 'needn't be this city, but I keep thinking that it has to be.' The pursuit of the dream will mean making a leap, getting on to new ground. The metaphor here feels exact. Yet, he says, even though he knows that the leap should be made, 'the old ground holds me. It holds us and holds us back.'

The pressures that hold back are not here articulated. What is it felt that may be lost in making the leap? The opposition to the new city is partially the self-interest of people like the speculator and builder John Dance who has no vision of Italianate hill-towns but thinks simply of developing new 'estates' which will increase his fortunes. But it is also old Mrs Lewis, the Prices' neighbour, who desperately fears the danger and despoliation which may come: 'She stared desperately into Susan's face. "Only I've been all my life here in Manod. I don't want to see it cut up... It'll be all cut up, all the fields around here. I don't want to see it."' And it is a response articulated by Matthew himself. He admits to Peter:

We drove here in September. On the road by Llanerch there's a black and white house, below a long dingle. The bracken begins just behind the house and there's a lane up under the trees, through a white field gate. It runs up under the gorse and the heather, and along the bank of the lane there are old grey marker stones, crusted with yellow lichen. I just stood there looking and I found myself saying: leave it alone, leave at least this place alone.

In his discussion of the poetry of John Clare, in *The Country and the City*, Williams identifies his own responses in similar terms. Clare's sense of loss in *Helpstone* is, he writes, explicitly about the 'dispossession of labour by capital', but it is 'set in a structure of feeling in which what wealth is most visibly destroying is "Nature": that complex of the land as it was, in the past and in childhood, which both ageing and alteration destroy.' Williams can, he writes 'recognize what Clare is describing: particular trees and a particular brook, by which I played as a child, have gone in just this way, in the past few years, in an improved use of marginal land.' But, and this I would argue, is a critical observation here, and one which is core to Williams' understanding of the relationship to land both in its material and abstract forms, 'It is... for any particular man... the loss of a specifically human and historical landscape, in which the source of feeling is not really that it is "natural" but that it is "native."' Here, and in a brief reference to *Anna Karenina*, Williams insists on the particular and known as driving motive. When Levin chooses physical labour 'it is in the end a choosing of people rather than of an abstract Nature – a choice of men to work with rather than a natural force in which to get lost.'

The Country and the City offers yet another way of understanding the 'old ground' and its pull. This is the need for the educationally promoted who, unlike Thomas Hardy's Jude, are allowed into the hallowed spaces of Christminster, to reject Christminster's judgement of 'the world of everyday work and of ordinary families' as unworthy of 'respect' or 'affection'. In his discussion of Hardy, Williams identifies important elements of Matthew's crisis:

> In Britain generally this is what has been happening: a moving out from old ways and places and ideas and feelings; a discovery in the new of certain unlooked-for problems, unexpected and very sharp crises, conflicts of desires and possibility.

The crisis that Matthew, on his return to Wales, is called upon to negotiate is the juxtaposition of a return to 'old ideas and feelings' and the challenge of the new that offers the possibility of real progress. In this novel, for the first time, a consciousness of a Welsh national interest is figured into the power relations of land both at the imaginary and at the material level.

Williams' relations with Wales at this time was advancing from the learning of its history which he had begun a decade earlier, to forming connections with people. The first half of *The Country and the City* and early chapters of *Manod* were written in the late sixties, the years when, as he says in *Politics and Letters*, he 'began having many more contacts with Welsh writers and intellectuals.' There was the physical move at this time in the taking of a cottage on the border to which he and Joy could retreat and where serious writing could be undertaken with less immediate interruption. Williams perhaps sums up his changing relations with the country when he says that he was coming to identify as a 'Welsh European'. Both the identifying adjective and the noun deserve attention, the latter as situating the former in crucial ways. The European is simultaneously a rejection of a certain kind of English culture and a claim to a wider grouping. He was not, he wrote in a brief essay on his reading practices 'part of orthodox English culture and social thought: not because it had not been available to me but because I had seen it and did not want it.' He insists that his fiction has little reference to that of his contemporaries, going on to state that when writing and rewriting *Border Country* he read hardly any other novels while *Second Generation* 'did not connect with other people's reading' and in England 'remained quite isolated'. His preferred writers are listed as Sartre, Solzhenitsyn, Kemal and Vonnegut. His interest in and admiration for Bahro, Gramsci and Benjamin is well attested.

European, then – and Welsh. 'Virtually all Welshmen ask themselves what it is to be Welsh,' Williams tells his interviewers in *Politics and Letters*, in a manner suggesting interrogation, of the concepts both of Wales and of Welsh identity. Wales in *Manod* is produced through dialogue between characters. Beth is one already noted, but there are others who have stayed in the country and rightly question the return of the native that is Matthew Price.

Far from any organic rootedness, Williams offers a Wales always in the making, and always contested. It is an idea of Wales that Gwyn A. Williams captured in his title, *When was Wales?*, and to which Raymond Williams responded by means of reviews of the new historiography then being written. In *Manod* the contested nature of Wales is offered in a conversation between Matthew and Plaid Cymru politician Tom Meurig. Matthew emphasises the 'mixed immigration' and consequent production of 'one of the strongest autonomous cultures in Europe' in industrial South Wales. Meurig insists on the 'strong native elements' of which the cultural base is now 'breaking up'. What might or should happen next, they both ask. Matthew acknowledges the emotional pull of a 'traditional rural Wales' but offers 'a quite alternative strategy' of sustaining a rural mid- Wales 'by organic development' and using major investment for the regeneration of the South Wales valleys. A range of possible futures for Wales is briefly outlined, but in this dialogue all remains in contestation: the history, the future and what it means to be Welsh. Matthew's claims to Welsh identity are dismissed by Meurig, 'You're not part of it. You're from the border. You live in both worlds, or in neither.' Yet not all those in Wales find Matthew's place of origin so dubious for earlier in the same chapter he has been offered the post as Director of a new Institute and Library of Industrial Wales, and in terms which clarify Wales as his country and as a country with a future. A letter informally expressing the offer reads,

We feel that it is wrong, that after so much struggle you should still be out of your country, and especially out of it now, when so much is happening here, so much new energy, so strong a sense of our possible future.

It is perhaps only the idea of Wales that at the end of *Manod* offers any note of even cautious optimism both individual and collective. Matthew accepts the post with the new Institute and declares his intention to continue to explore the potential of the Manod project. However, now working not with a London-centred network of power between state and business but using 'all the work and the thinking that is being done' in Wales and which was excluded from the official files with which he was, as consultant, presented. Behind all the wheeling and dealing, the deception and obfuscation of the project of a new model of a city, lies the germ of a possibility, the exploration of 'new social patterns, new actual social relations.' However, Manod offers no closure, there is no resolution, no forward path that will necessarily lead to the disputed land of this new city, to be reclaimed for Wales. There is only the 'dream of a country', possible through ordinary people like Modlen who at the end mops out the floor retreating out through the door as Matthew and Susan leave the cottage rented for the purpose of the consultancy. The discussions and the debate will return, but Williams makes no concession to cosy certainty as to their direction or end.

The emphasis in the dream is always on process. Even as Matthew insists to Tom Meurig on the 'mixed immigration' of the coalfields, so Williams insists that all communities, even those seemingly less vulnerable to change, are necessarily always in process. His essays and speeches are threaded with references to diversity. In a presidential address to the Classical Association in Cardiff he insists on the recognition of 'the facts of actual change and diversity' as 'necessary grounds for wisdom in complex and contending societies.' Neither is it easy to find in his fiction or non-fiction much evidence for a view of Wales that is complacent or mired in the past. The consistent emphases are of a society in process, of the values of diversity, of social practices and pure ideas which are produced by a specific history. The communities and settlements, settle being another key word for Williams, of his fiction are surprisingly mobile. Even *Border Country*, seemingly the most settled of the novels fits surprisingly well into Patrick Parrinder's category of 'immigrant literature', where 'the children of immigrants re-imagine the lives of their parents.' Its story-time opens with the arrival of Harry and Ellen in the village of Glynmawr, their expressed need, in the exact terms 'to make a settlement'. The characters are, in the terms identified by Parrinder, 'held in a highly specific local space, or what the language of imperialism would call a settlement or outpost.' *Second Generation* is explicitly a novel of the Welsh diaspora and *Manod* a place shown to be in dire need of immigration.

This process and mobility may be seen as significant to Williams' social vision. Even without the planned immigration which would be brought about by the building of the new city, *Manod* demonstrates the process of change, the continuing mixed immigration which is taking place in rural Wales. On a visit to the small town of Nantlais, which it is planned will be part of the new city, Matthew is conscious that the old properties are being bought by

> a new kind of settler who saw in mid-Wales one of the last accessible places of calm: a place to work in new ways, to practise crafts, experiment in life styles. Along the main street there were already nine of these new enterprises: a bookshop, a print and map shop, three shops selling antiques, a pottery, two woollen craft shops and a health food store.

Although Matthew does not comment on these changes, the emphasis on calm and creativity implies a measure of approbation. The essay 'Between Country and City' suggests Williams' response as consistent with that of Matthew. It records the changes in 'the occupations of my neighbours within five miles of my house in the Black Mountains: the incomers who are 'weavers and knitters; potters; cabinet-maker; pine-furniture makers, writers, sculptors, restaurateurs…' These 'comparatively recent immigrants' he sees as vital 'in restoring a genuine fabric of rural society.'

There is an argument to be made that the Welsh societies of Williams' fiction and with which his essays are concerned, rural or based on working-class communities in the mining valleys, remain narrow and traditional in focus. James A. Davies reads Williams' fictional oeuvre as one of steady decline caused by his exile. Even the distance from

Wales is seen as crucial: 'The narrator of *Border Country* resembles a Welshman influenced by years of academic life *on the far side of England.*' (emphasis added). Williams had, argues Davies, 'been away from Wales for too long and misunderstood… the effects of exile.' Williams' Wales is 'a concept of limited geographical and social range… Commercial Wales, intellectual Wales, bourgeois Wales, urban and suburban Wales hardly feature in [his] vision.' This argument has some force. Although Williams' essays and speeches abound with acknowledgements of the educational work and achievements in the Welsh valleys in the early and mid-twentieth century, the Welsh trilogy may have an under-representation of working-class activists or professionals engaging in wider intellectual debate, and unarguably the terms in which he chooses to construct his fictional Wales are highly specific. Yet the 1975 essay 'Welsh Culture', written during the period of *Manod's* long gestation, opens with an acknowledgement that culture can be understood as 'a way of life determined by the National Coal Board, the British Steel Corporation, the Milk Marketing Board, the Co-op and Marks and Spencers, the BBC…' It is also evident that the wider range of characters is to the fore in *The Volunteers* and *Loyalties*, where activists and radical intellectuals are a significant presence.

In a late interview with Terry Eagleton, Williams talks of the experience of Welsh identity as one of ambiguity and contradiction, and one can read his own relation to Wales in these terms. In 'Welsh Culture' he writes of different tendencies living in 'the same bodies, the same minds.' One of the tendencies, labelled as accommodation, is clearly to be rejected, the fake historical costume past of 'bardism and druidism' and the playing up of difference and weaknesses for commercial entertainment. But what of the others, the 'proud and dignified withdrawal to Fortress Wales: the old times, the old culture, the still living enclave' or the move from the enclave into the reality of a modern Welsh culture?

Withdrawal suggests a retreat, a decision to disengage with the tumult of the contemporary and the political which is far from appropriate to the embattled Williams. Yet the idea of return is more appropriate and persuasive to his reading, his writing and his living. The account that he gives of his reading practice opens with the comment that 'there were very few books in our house when I was a child.' All these he read 'with the kind of over-and-over reading, I have never, with certain books, lost as a habit.' The same pattern of return marks his writing. His commentaries on those writers with whose situations and responses he finds most affinities, such as George Eliot, Hardy and Lawrence, re-use the same terms and ideas. The echoes and partial echoes convey not the sense of a writer saving intellectual effort by giving a quick brush down to an old set of the notes from the filing cabinet, but rather of one who needs to revisit those writers and issues which are of primary importance, to re-examine earlier responses and to recast them in a form more effective or exact. He goes back over and over because it is *this* that matters. The subject for Williams the novelist is pre-eminently the return of the native: the narrative of the son who abandons his place of origin but, unable to make that escape permanent, returns to the settlement.

During the period of the writing of *Manod* and *The Country and the City* he and Joy bought a cottage at Craswall in the Black Mountains. Craswall lies in the Olchon Valley, which opens close to Pandy. The significant elements of the landscape are those which marked the landscape of his childhood and which structure the landscape of *Border Country*. An account of the Olchon Valley in Owen Sheers' 2007 novel, *Resistance*, demonstrates this, beginning with the figure of the shape of a hand, used by Williams to open his last work *People of the Black Mountains*,

> If [Sarah] were to follow her mother's description of the Black Mountains Hand, then where she rode now was in the hollow between thumb and forefinger, The Hatterall Ridge, on her right, was the forefinger, a long slice of land pointing south-east towards Pandy... a view right down to the distant island-hills of Skirrid Fawr and Mynydd Merddin rising from the lowland fields...

Suggestively, Sheers comments that 'No-one came into this valley by accident. You only ever came here if you needed to, and apart from those who lived here, few people ever did.' This is indeed border country but, interestingly, it lies on the English side of the border. Williams came here because he needed to: this, for him, as he writes in his discussion of Clare, is the native, the 'specifically human and historical landscape.' So, how important is the border itself, as distinct from the border country?

In terms of the frontiers this valley is an ambiguous place. Williams' grave is in the extension of the churchyard at Clodock, from Craswall the nearest available consecrated spot, and, like the cottage, in the county of Herefordshire. He lies therefore in England but surrounded by David Lewis, Evan Evans, the Joneses, the Griffithes, the Watkins and the Gwatkins, while the churchwarden, who has never moved from that valley and is English, speaks with a distinctive Welsh accent. Historically it is a place of ambiguous status, originally the Hundred of Ewias in Wales until boundary changes in the reign of Henry VIII, after which it continued as part of the Welsh Church until 1858 when it was included in the diocese of Hereford. If Craswall's national identity has been fluid, so was that of the Monmouthshire where Williams grew up, although he makes no reference to this peculiarity. The county was then not indisputably in Wales but a strange place known as 'Wales and Monmouthshire', where the players of one of the rugby clubs, Newport, were eligible for selection by either the Welsh or the English international team, where it was possible to attend a primary school and to celebrate St David's Day but to sing the Welsh national anthem in English.

The return is to the native place, the allegiance to the border country. He was, before, during and after the period of *Manod, The Country and The City* and the return to the Black Mountains, setting out and developing a case for the absolute value of the specific, the material and the local, where human welfare is understood to be intimately connected with the good of the animate and inanimate with which it shares space against what David Harvey has called 'the deracinated politics of neo-liberalism.' But his work demonstrates an equally powerful need to negotiate the relation of the particular to wider networks, a negotiation that is demonstrated most evidently in the speech 'Socialism and Ecology' given to SERA, the Socialist Environment and Resources Association, of which he was vice-president, in 1982. It is this refusal of any false binary between the local and the global which clarifies Williams' position in terms of the dream of a country which is central to *Manod*. This is certainly no withdrawal into an enclave but a desire to negotiate and help to construct the reality of a modern Welsh culture with possibility of new social relations and patterns of living.

Raymond Williams

Border Country, 1960, Library of Wales, Parthian, 2006.

Second Generation, Chatto and Windus, 1964.

The Country and the City, 1973, Spokesman, 2011.

Television, Technology and Cultural Form, 1974, Routledge Classics, 2003.

The Fight for Manod, 1979, Hogarth, 1988.

Politics and Letters, 1979, Verso, 2015.

Socialism and Ecology, Socialist Environment and Resources Association, 1983.

'Writing, Speech and the Classical' in *What I Came to Say*, Hutchinson, 1989.

'Welsh Culture' and 'The Social Significance of 1926' in *Who Speaks for Wales? Raymond Williams*, edited Daniel Williams, UWP, 2003.

For the account by Raymond Williams of his reading practices, see Frederic Raphael ed. *Bookmarks*, London: Cape, 1975.

Other works

James A. Davies 'Not Going Back, but Exile Ending' in *Raymond Williams: Politics, Education and Letters*, 1993.

Terry Eagleton 'Raymond Williams: Communities and Universities' *Keywords: A Journal of Cultural Materialism*, 1998.

David Harvey *Spaces of Capital: Towards a Critical Geography*, Edinburgh University Press, 2001.

Kenneth O. Morgan *Rebirth of a Nation: A History of Modern Wales*, Oxford University Press, 1981.

Patrick Parrinder, *Nation and Novel*, Oxford University Press, 2008.

6

The Purposes of Adult Education

Derek Tatton

The book likely to stand as the most thorough and comprehensive collection of Williams' writings on adult education, with exceptionally helpful commentaries and views on Williams' contribution to education, has the title *Border Country – Raymond Williams in Adult Education,* edited by John McIlroy and Sallie Westwood, and published in 1993.

The title *From Wales to the World* is pertinent because probably the most significant lacuna in the McIlroy and Westwood book is the absence of Wales and, in fact, despite the book's title, they make little or no reference to Williams' *Border Country* background. This is quite understandable because Williams' long formative years in adult education were experienced entirely in south-east England and his engagement with the central issues regarding educational aims, curricula and teaching were, quite literally, English. It was mainly English literature he taught, or at least works translated into English. More than that, it was the very English Oxford/Workers' Educational Association tutorial tradition which dominated the theoretical and practical debates within, and about, adult education. Hence, scholars and educationalists going through the records, when writing biographically about those years, will naturally engage with this emphasis on that history and culture within adult education.

McIlroy justifies his chapter title, 'The Unknown Raymond Williams', convincingly,

> The flood of literature since his untimely death... has had very little to say about Williams' life and work during the immediate post-war years when he was a tutor in adult education. Yet in important ways these years were the making of Raymond Williams...

We can revisit now that still often *forgotten* Williams, helped especially by two books with an evidently strong Welsh connection and emphasis which, with the social and political impact of devolution, foregrounds Williams' own self-defining claim to be a 'Welsh European'. Dai Smith's *A Warrior's Tale* (2008) draws out and explores the complexity of his subject. The man is, in himself, complicated and the book offers remarkable testimony to a paradox at the heart of Williams' project. Where most of his readers place much more value on his non-fiction work, Williams stressed his commitment to, and the value he gave to, writing fiction. This paradox is relevant to our theme here, as will be explored later. The other fine book drawn on, *Changing Lives – WEA in Wales 1907–2007*, provides detailed evidence of the exceptionally rich adult education in that country, distinctive for its own conflicts and tensions. A further oversight of this forgotten Williams is the productivity of those years in adult learning when he wrote *Reading and Criticism*; *Drama from Ibsen to Eliot*; *Drama in Performance*; *Culture and Society*; *The Long Revolution*; much fiction, and later books central to his project, notably *Keywords*. Most of these books were, he readily acknowledges, stimulated by his adult education teaching and experience.

This early detachment from an academic career was a very conscious decision. After he sat his examinations he applied and was appointed to a post with the Oxford Extra-Mural Delegacy in conjunction with the Workers' Education Association (WEA), based in south-east England, as Dai Smith states, 'Following his First he had an offer from Trinity of £200 a year as Senior Scholar… but he wanted to move on… (to) adult education and writing… It all promised to be rather more fulfilling… than any conventional academic work, even a research degree under the admired Leavis.'

He was not alone at that time in making this kind of decision, of course. Richard Hoggart and Edward Thompson are just two of his best-known contemporaries to follow the same path. The adult education movement in the forties and fifties seemed to offer real opportunities for progressive graduates to combine continued academic study with work within an educational movement linked to universities, but with a history of challenge and even hostility to orthodox state-funded university teaching and adult education.

This produced tensions which Dai Smith writes about at length comparing Williams to colleagues within the Oxford Delegacy notably, Thomas Hodgkin 'about as well-connected an Oxonian as could be' and a member of the Communist Party from 1938 to 1949; Frank Pickstock, son of a North Staffordshire miner, who worked as a railway booking clerk before involvement in the WEA and the Labour Party, and 'Hodgkin's polar opposite, in both tastes and outlook. Only Adult Education united them.'

Dai Smith develops the theme:

Raymond Williams, not for the first or last time, made no easy alliances. If Pickstock, from a similar background, was someone with whom he could work through the 1950s with a mutual, if guarded, respect, it was Hodgkin, with his bolder belief that working-class education needed to be rooted in wider working-class institutions and taught by 'committed socialists', who touched Williams' instincts for education as a process of social change, not just the purveying of training skills and intellectual objectivity. Not that these tensions surfaced only in Williams; there was a long history of conflict between the explicitly Marxist National Council of Labour Colleges established in 1921 to provide independent working-class education, and the WEA, thought by many to offer a route to incorporation rather than release for working-class students. In practice, even where the divisions were most sharply articulated, as in South Wales, students did not always make such a clear distinction and were inclined to sample or even sate themselves on the wares of both. Nor, in 1945, is there any evidence that Williams would be more than mildly aware of this past history. But there was, indeed, the rub for those on the Left, not all Communists, who set out to claim a part of the WEA tradition for explicit political ends and, in savage fashion, were rebuffed. Where Williams fitted in to all that puzzled some at the time; always, it seemed, there was the difficulty, in any context of relationships that were both political and personal, of elucidating his exact position.

This chapter seeks to tease out several issues from this, helped by Williams himself given that he wrote extensively and at different periods on these tensions, political and personal, making it clear that he did not have an 'exact position' on this history because of a deep ambivalence about the core WEA mission.

Let us begin by taking the quote above: 'Nor, in 1945, is there any evidence that Williams could be more than mildly aware of this past history.' As historian and biographer, Dai Smith will know about any lack of 'evidence' on this, but taking another approach and working from Williams' constant emphasis on 'lived experience' and the importance of 'roots', the argument can take a different form and direction. Coming from Wales, absorbing from a very young age the whole culture in part through his father's local social and political involvement, we can go back to consider that history of the Welsh WEA, the Labour Colleges and Coleg Harlech gaining insights into where the young Jim, his boyhood home name, came from in this special sphere and the impact these roots had upon the maturing Raymond.

The twenty years or so before the First World War were among the most decisive in modern Welsh history, and adult education played a full part in the drama of these years. South Wales was a society, combining extraordinary dynamism with immigration and rapid industrial growth – as documented in John Davies' fine and authoritative *A History of Wales*, first published two years after Williams died. Davies writes eloquently about how Keir Hardie, a Scot, who was 'able to strike a note which appealed to Welsh voters' when 'in 1900 Merthyr was the sole constituency in the UK to return a convinced socialist'... 'He praised the attributes of the Celts, adopting as his slogan 'The Red Dragon and the Red Flag'. By 1920, there were 290,000 coal miners in this region. Dai Smith's description 'a dystopia aspiring to utopia', conveys the contradictions: turmoil, along with Welsh roots helping the formation of quite stable communities, literate, musical, politically sophisticated. Tonypandy in 1910 experienced a long serious industrial dispute, iconic for its dramatic embrace of theories of workers' control, syndicalism within an intense and vivid Welsh culture.

Out of the growing industrial unrest, there emerged a new pattern of independent adult education. After the famous strike at Ruskin College, Oxford in 1909, the adult education movement split and the foundation of Plebs led eventually to the National Council of Labour Colleges (NCLC). The circumstances surrounding the Ruskin strike had a significant impact on Welsh adult education and social history as the battle between the *Plebs* and the WEA became one of the most dramatic features of the time. It was not difficult to see that here the great issues of Welsh politics were expressed in microcosm. Richard Lewis, in *Changing Lives,* conveys an important emphasis:

> … it is crucial to see that throughout these early years a 'highly plastic political continuum' stretched right across the 'progressive alliance'.

A feel for what Lewis is describing can be captured with reference to colourful individuals like Peter Wright: a prominent local political figure with radical and Labour connections – a Scotsman who had migrated to South Wales during the great expansion of the coalfield in the late nineteenth century and became a moderately successful businessman in the coal shipping trade of Newport. Wright was an advocate of state and local authority action to promote the welfare of working people; willing to court support amongst the advocates of 'independent' Labour representation, he spoke regularly on the platforms of the Independent Labour Party.

The 'progressive alliance' had fewer women, of course, but it did include Miss Elizabeth Hughes 'one of the most remarkable Welsh women of her age…' She was certainly middle class but described her politics as 'Radical and

Democrat'. She travelled extensively, living for a period in Japan, and was an acknowledged expert on American educational developments. In 1899 following a very distinguished career in teacher education (first Principal of Cambridge College for the Training of Women Teachers), she retired to her home town of Barry to devote her life to promoting the social and educational improvement of working people in general and women in particular. She represented Glamorgan County education committee on the WEA provisional committee and remained a major figure in the work of the WEA in South Wales until her death in 1925.

Noah Ablett, from Wales, had played a prominent part as a dissident Ruskin student and in creating the Plebs movement. He challenged the WEA's links to the universities and the idea of an impartial education. This was not the route to be followed by the workers who needed an educational organisation, independent of universities and state. Guided by Ablett the movement's chief theorist and publicist, the Plebs developed apace in South Wales. After the Ruskin strike and the establishment of the residential Central Labour College, the greatest success of the South Wales Plebs was the support they gained from miners in the region. Several districts of the South Wales Miners Federation decided to support the Central College, before in 1914 The Fed, as it was popularly known, took over maintenance with the National Union Railwayman. In 1914, six of the twelve residential students were members of The Fed.

The WEA, however, had also taken root in Wales. The first Welsh branch was formed in Barry in 1906, and then in 1907 an autonomous South Wales region came into being. By 1914, the WEA could claim to be a broadly based movement. It had clear support from some labour organisations; several co-operative societies had affiliated as had some important trades councils and, significantly, some lodges and districts of The Fed. However, it was weaker than it might have been. The Plebs and the Central Labour College had seen to that. The rivalry between the Labour College movement and the WEA was manifest throughout Britain at this time, but the struggle was more intense and bitter in South Wales than in any other area. The mature Williams was well aware of this as is very clear from *Politics and Letters:* 'The NCLC in certain areas was a more important movement. In South Wales it produced far more educated militants than the WEA ever did.'

The success of the NCLC created widespread prejudice against all official or semi-official adult education agencies. This is the essential background, along with WEA support, from which flows the distinctive history of Coleg Harlech in North Wales. The early history of that institution (where Raymond Williams from the 1960s gave occasional lectures) helps signpost the connections, personal, historical and political and a biographical sketch of two founders illustrates the 'plastic continuum'.

Thomas Jones' life and his social and political views offer fascinating insights into Welsh political and educational history. He was born in 1870 in Rhymney, a mining village in South Wales. His father was a company storekeeper and the family were bilingual and strictly nonconformist. He went to grammar school and felt that the 'pulpit was my manifest destiny'. He left school at 14, and it was several years before he became a student at the University College of Wales, Aberystwyth. The centre of the linguistic, cultural and political revival, Aberystwyth gave him a new sense of Wales which he never lost.

This was the age of Charles Booth, Beatrice Webb and Keir Hardie, when there was new interest in social philosophies, and Jones moved 'from evangelism to the study of social questions' and from 'Liberalism to Labour'. From Aberystwyth he moved to Glasgow where, as a student, 'he became fully imbued with the neo-Hegelian ideals that pervaded the intellectual climate of the time.' His subsequent experiences of Glasgow made clear to him the nature of trade unionism and he was later to write: '... the inherent weakness of trade unionism was quite clear in the 1880s, it was a negotiating and fighting force, but it could not give us socialism. Along with the progress of the unions had come a dangerous sectionalising spirit.' The theme was revisited when, after returning to Wales, he addressed miners in his native Rhymney Valley, calling for a broadening of perspectives, a vision of wider social objectives, and for unions to throw their weight on the side of character and education. He later wrote, as his daughter Eirene White records in her biographical booklet, 'My religion is education... It is a way to the kingdom of heaven... the object of adult education is to break down the barriers which hinder the masses of the people from enjoying these riches.' That is of course, a vision remarkably close to the view of the WEA held by its founder Albert Mansbridge. The idealism and the radicalism of Jones' Welsh nonconformist background had been channelled into Fabian progressivism, but this was an ideological perspective that did not sit easily with the younger working-class leadership of South Wales Labour. The WEA was a key organisation, and it was at its meetings that he met a group who were to dominate adult education in Wales.

By the twenties, through the popularity and the success of the Summer Schools, the work of Ruskin College and the Central Labour College, the time was ripe for a residential college in Wales. George Davison was the other key figure who played a crucial role. After working in the Exchequer and the Audit Department of the Treasury, George Davison had become a pioneering photographer and the Managing Director of Kodak. He was not, however, a conventional Edwardian bourgeois millionaire. By the time he moved up to North Wales, he had become a philosophical anarchist, deeply influenced by Kropotkin and Tolstoy.

Jones met Davison at a Fabian Summer School at Llanbedr in 1909. They became close friends, though Jones was fully aware of Davison's views and activities. In 1913 he told Jones that,

... all these under-currents of anarchism interest me: in Drama, Music, Painting and the industrial movement. Right out of their own experience is being evolved the workers' distrust of leadership and officialdom of every type – the authoritarian domination from above (Gods, priests, academics, states, Labour leaders, TUCs, Parliament etc) and so they must come to think and speak for themselves.

Davison was living at *Wern Fawr* (the House and Hall) in Harlech during the years of increased trade union militancy in South Wales and, indeed, he became directly involved in working-class politics.

At Ammanford in the anthracite coalfield there emerged in the aftermath of the 1910 and 1911 industrial conflict a distinctive group, influenced in part by the Independent Labour Party, and the anarcho-syndicalism that characterised the Plebs in South Wales. There were similar groups in several South Wales centres, but what distinguished the Ammanford Group was their acquisition in 1913 of an old vicarage and the conversion of this into a reading room, library and meeting place. Davison, now a 'philosophic anarchist' bought the house, financed the conversion and helped to stock the library which included works by Kropotkin and Gustave Herve (at that time an anti-militarist socialist and pacifist – he later became an admirer of Mussolini). The old vicarage, newly painted white, named *The White House* after Davison's home beside the Thames was promoted as a discussion centre. The group maintained close links with the National Council of Labour Colleges and the Plebs movement and were involved in the politics of the area. In the war years, *The White House* became the centre of Independent Labour Party and anti-militarist agitation in the district. After the war, the House became the centre for trade union activity for the Ammanford area.

Davison left Harlech and, in 1922, went to Juan Les Pins on the French Riviera (for health reasons). With *Wern Fawr* vacant and private sale proving difficult, Davison wrote to Jones (in March 1923) asking for his help, to get the idea of purchase fully considered particularly amongst the South Wales activists. Jones said that he and Silyn Roberts (who later became Secretary of the North Wales WEA) had long wanted to save it for workers' education. It took three years of negotiations and fund-raising to launch Coleg Harlech, which opened in October 1927. Thus, the College was founded and established precisely at the moment when industrial Wales was experiencing the most bitter and intense confrontation between Capital and Labour: the period of the General Strike and the six-month lockout of the miners. Furthermore, Coleg Harlech embodied all the contradictions, ironies and tensions in its very conception and birth: funded by capital raised from capitalists for a workers' college, sited in a mansion in scenic North Wales, far from the industrial centres of South Wales yet with the most direct links – at all levels – to those centres.

This criss-crossing of struggles for funding and independence emerging from ideological, religious and cultural divisions is the context from which to now return to Williams' personal journey in adult education. Dai Smith quoting from the unpublished novel *The Grasshoppers* (1955), refers to Williams' view on the untrustworthiness of biographies because they impose a pattern on a life's development:

'Only the line of a life, hardly anything of its area can be articulated…' This can be applied to Williams himself, most notably when contrasting his fiction with the other writing. His fiction is Welsh located, conscious and aware throughout, and it is interesting and maybe significant that Labour College activists feature as in *Second Generation,* with shop steward Harold Owen poring over his NCLC correspondence course, and Mark Evans, MP in *The Volunteers,* who was a Labour College organiser before becoming Deputy Director of the Extra-Mural Department of the University of Wales, Brecon. Therefore, whilst working for the WEA, and very committed to its history, in Williams' fiction it is the Labour College movement that features.

His non-fiction books and articles only reveal a more conscious Welshness much later. Dai Smith comments again on the paradox that he lived most of his life in England but the life of the mind, of which his fiction was most revealing, ever took him back to the Black Mountains. He later famously defined himself as a 'Welsh European' but as early as 1949 in his unpublished novel *Brynllwyd* he was engaging in self-analysis on the meaning for him of 'Welshness' and the 'English tradition'. Talking about his novel, *The Fight for Manod,* with his New Left Review interviewers in 1978, he says he wants '… the Welsh people – still a radical and cultured people – to defeat, override or bypass bourgeois England.' He sought connections across Europe with 'my kind of people; the people I come from and belong to, and my more conscious Welshness is, as I feel it, my way of learning those connections.' As Dai Smith puts it right at the beginning of his biography, 'With a late exasperation in 1979, he would insist that in England the holistic effort of his work was not readily appreciated and that only in Wales did he have a sense that there was an appreciation of its unity.'

In *Warrior* Smith locates the continuity and unity of that consciousness in Raymond's family and community experience and most directly, of course, through his father. Williams himself recalled that his father's first job after the Great War had been 'right down in the mining valleys which were very political, with a fairly advanced socialist culture.' Dai Smith continues, 'Harry Williams lived more or less permanently in this maelstrom, where syndicalists and communists were the kind of minority activists that supporters of the Labour Party were elsewhere in Britain…' For Harry working in Aberdare,

> this was a proletarian world almost out of a textbook. Its power and its strength would be acknowledged later by the son who would both theorise about its potential and *imagine its distinctiveness in his fiction*, (my emphasis) but only the father would ever have personal knowledge of one of the great European bastions of an industrial working class at its zenith.

Williams added that when 'he moved home to the border again, he had acquired its perspectives.'

The formation and making then of our Celtic radical had deep roots. Everything Williams said, wrote and did within the adult education movement illustrates his intimate knowledge of the tensions around 'independent workers education'. It is hard to believe that such an exceptionally precocious young man in the late 1930s was not already quite well-informed of the historical background of Welsh adult education. As soon as he became involved as a tutor from 1945 onwards, it is clear from the record of his teaching and writing, that he built up and absorbed a wide knowledge and experience. He was more aware than most that the pedagogy of the NCLC shared some of the weaknesses of the WEA. Especially in his early years as an adult tutor, Williams revealed a radical approach to teaching, championing a discussion method. In his own words,

> The authority it creates is not that of the students or of the tutor, but of the embodied class – the group. The process of his authority and the manner of tutorial class education is what I call discussion…

However, the lecture remained unchallenged as a conventional and standard method of teaching. For the NCLC this could mean syllabuses tightly organised so that students could move from 'Primitive Communism', by ten weekly lectures, to 'Capitalism Today'. Subjects were rigidly demarcated and formed a hierarchy of knowledge organised around a 'base' and 'superstructure' model; an equivalent to the 'social purpose' philosophy of the WEA, which had an almost identical hierarchy of subjects. Hence, we can be sure that Williams shared the view of the NCLC's most perceptive historian, Stuart Macintyre, when he wrote, 'We may generalize by saying that the WEA classes bore the characteristics of their locality and that in some areas where Marxism was strong, the gulf between the Labour Colleges and the WEA was not great.'

Williams' stance on this did not waver greatly throughout, but he did move steadily and sympathetically towards the Labour College position on the vital issues of 'independence'. When reviewing William W. Craik's book, *The Central Labour College* in 1965 he wrote,

> At a time when we are again actively discussing the future of adult and workers' education… (the) book is especially welcome… the current argument about the organisation of workers' education which though given little publicity is of fundamental importance… This vigorous justification of a prolonged campaign and a tenacious principle needs to be read by many outside the particular field of adult education.

That was a theme he addressed at greater length in a characteristically eloquent newspaper article. The *Guardian* essay of 1968 entitled, '*Different Sides of the Wall*', begins with a personal anecdote about a miner in an Oxford museum during a break in the WEA summer school literature group on 'the importance of work, not written about enough.' This led him to a review of student power in adult learning,

> for good historical reasons… generation after generation they insisted on sharing the essential decisions: about

what was to be studied and how. Repeatedly, they set up their own institutions, and in this kind of self-organising there was always a close relation between education and democracy… the relation between learning and what it was for… The corresponding societies, the Hampden clubs, the secular Sunday schools, the cooperative circles, the mechanics' institutes, the Workers' Education Association, the labour colleges: we can learn more, now, from these, about the crisis in education, than from the more formal established institutions. For there was always a tension, of a most complicated kind. Some people have always wanted to control them (it was often easy, through finance) so that what was taught was what the authorities decided.

'Tension, of a most complicated kind…' A tension too in Williams, further inspection of which helps address Dai Smith's puzzle and paradox. The episode that demonstrates most clearly Williams' close awareness of and ambivalence about the ideological conflict between NCLC/CP positions and the WEA occurred early in the Cold War. It is described in Roger Fieldhouse's *Adult Education and the Cold War* (1985). The following summary takes us through to Williams' own exceptionally revealing commentary upon it.

The united front politics of the war and 1945 led to an ideological climate which was less implacably hostile to communism. Even so, divisions were there, below the surface. The General Secretary during this period, Ernest Green, was a zealous defender of WEA's relationship with trade unions, hostile to the NCLC and intolerant of communist or left-wing movements and views. Thus, the presence of Thomas Hodgkin in the key position of Secretary to the Delegacy from June 1945, with a rapidly expanding team of Oxford tutors working for the WEA, offered potential for ideological tensions as the Cold War polarized and made more frigid the political positions.

At a meeting of the Oxford Tutorial Classes Committee in June 1948, Green proposed an enquiry into allegations related to certain trade union conferences and courses held in Oxford and courses at the Wedgwood Memorial College, Barlaston. His proposal accepted, a report was presented in March 1949. From then on an apprehensive atmosphere prevailed in the Delegacy as a whole, but especially in the WEA North Staffordshire District where tensions heightened, when Frank Pickstock became the Secretary of the Tutorial Classes Committee and, in his own words, 'was then in complete control'. Pickstock and Hodgkin agreed that there followed a deepening 'cold war' polarization, Hodgkin said, 'One was conscious of this cold wind blowing through the Delegacy, but it was blowing through the world at the same time.' The Barlaston affair left a legacy of bitterness and Hodgkin believed the appointment of tutors became an increasingly politicised process.

Raymond Williams lived and worked mostly in south-east England during this period, but as a member of the Delegacy, he was well aware of what was happening and, indeed, he was involved in the dispute. He refers to this 'sharp form of the Cold War' in the interviews, *Politics and Letters*, 'The whole Delegacy was seen as a Communist

cell. There was a violent assault on its whole organization
and on Hodgkin in particular. There was an extreme crisis
within the institution during the late 40s and early 50s. It
was a sharp local form of the Cold War.'

A more revealing account of the conflict was given in
an article Williams wrote for the 100 edition of New Left
Review:

> I remember an extraordinary experience during the
> Cold War when the institution I worked in was almost
> evenly divided between CP members... and Labour Party
> members. For internal reasons it became very bitter, and
> there was both intrigue and witch-hunting. It was a curious
> phenomenon that at the worst moments I was the only
> person to whom both sides spoke: the Communists
> because I shared their intellectual perspectives and most
> of their political positions; the non-Communists – but
> there's the rub – because I, like almost all of them, was
> from a working-class family... I joined neither camp, but
> I remember the experience, and I remember it especially
> when any later generation, coming from where it will,
> starts using either form of contradictory rhetoric; either,
> 'these bloody Communist (Marxist) intellectuals' or, on
> the other hand, the more abstract diagnoses of vulgarism,
> corporatism, workerism or populism.

This chapter has elaborated an argument for Williams'
lived experience of the tensions within the 'adult education
movement'. He wrote, as we have seen, extensively and at

different periods on these tensions, both political and personal, making it clear that he did not have an 'exact position' on this history because of a deep ambivalence about the core WEA mission. McIlroy's carefully researched account of Williams' Adult Education Tutor experience unfortunately makes very few references, as I have underlined, to Williams' Welsh background. He does though offer this explanation for Raymond's warmth to Frank Pickstock, 'Williams' roots in Welsh working-class community meant he sometimes felt at home with those on the right such as Frank Pickstock who, like Williams' father, had been a railwayman and a participant in the General Strike.' The reason, it has been argued here, why during the Cold War conflict, Williams could be at home with those on the right and the left in the adult education movement, relates to his formation within the 'highly plastic continuum' across the progressive alliance in South Wales. 'The only person to whom both sides spoke' as he put it, already knew of conflict over not only content, but method of teaching and it was perhaps this awareness that gave intellectual support for his refusal to take sides. The Celtic radical, whose personality and character had those roots, was as acutely aware as anyone of the creative tensions between Pickstock and Hodgkin, and from which he fashioned the political and intellectual confidence to embrace WEA and NCLC perspectives as a critical friend.

Raymond Williams

'Notes on Marxism in Britain from 1945', *New Left Review* 100, November 1976 – January 1977.

Politics and Letters, 1979, Verso, 2015.

Border Country – Raymond Williams in Adult Education, edited McIlroy and Sallie Westwood, NIACE, 1993.

Who Speaks for Wales? Raymond Williams, edited Daniel Williams, UWP, 2003.

Other works

John Davies, *A History of Wales*, UWP/Allen Lane, 1993.

Joe England ed, *Changing Lives: Workers' Education in Wales, 1907–2007,* Llafur, 2007.

Roger Fieldhouse, *Adult Education and the Cold War*, Leeds University Department of Adult and Continuing Education, 1985.

Stuart Macintyre, *A Proletarian Science*, Cambridge University Press, 1980.

Dai Smith, *Raymond Williams: A Warrior's Tale*, Parthian, 2008.

Peter Stead, *Coleg Harlech – The First Fifty Years*, UWP, 1977.

E. White, *Thomas Jones*, Aberystwyth, c.1975.

7

Welsh European

Hywel Dix

In developing the body of work now known as cultural materialism Raymond Williams was contributing to a wealth of cultural theory across Europe. The work mediated through history, literature, linguistics, sociology, anthropology and beyond, but cannot be reduced to any of these. We may, however, identify common arguments and ideas that make for what was distinctive about the work and how he developed it; and so locate the writing in this broader European dialogue. In seeking to summarise discerning tendencies in Williams' thinking, it is possible to identify four main elements:

- The use of history as means of apprehending the possibility for intervention and change in the cultural politics of the present.
- The need to relate individual forms of material production

to the varying and intersecting social formations in which they are both determined and active.

- The refusal to assign strict and sole social causality to the system of economic relations.
- The apprehension that language acquisition and language use are material and social processes, capable of balancing structure and agency in a highly complex and dialectical way.

In print, Williams' discussion of each of these elements is often maintained at a highly impersonal and abstract level; often referring to the work of his contemporaries only by means of indirect allusion rather than through explicit engagement with published works. To uncover those tracks of theoretical abstraction in Williams' work, the chapter attempts to restore a sense of latent dialogue by making more explicit than Williams the nature of that engagement with European theory, especially in the work of Louis Althusser* and Lucien Goldmann†. Emphasis then moves to the gradual process by which his best-known concepts were worked out over time as his sense of being a Welsh European deepened.

In meeting these aims, the chapter will begin with a consideration of the relationship of Williams' work to that of Althusser and Goldmann. It then explores how Williams

---

* Louis Althusser was a philosopher of extraordinary influence and key figure in French structuralism.
† Lucien Goldmann was a philosopher and sociologist, and professor in Paris.

met the work of contemporaries in the development of his own practice by comparing his early *Drama From Ibsen to Eliot* (1952) with its amended version *Drama From Ibsen to Brecht* (1968), when his practice of cultural materialism had matured. Finally, it examines the development of Williams' sophisticated concepts for the analysis of culture alongside subsequent European thinkers, most notably Jürgen Habermas[‡] and Pierre Bourdieu[§]. This tripartite structure, moving from European theorists to Williams and back again, will underline the manner of Williams' debate with critical writers by emphasizing both how he developed his own thinking through that encounter and how his work contributed to the development of others'.

Raymond Williams once acknowledged that a visit by Lucien Goldmann to Cambridge in 1970 was an important moment in the development of his critical thinking (*Problems in Materialism and Culture*). Goldmann represented to Williams a significant advance in contemporary French thinking, and his idea of genetic structuralism, which balances structure with agency, parallels much of Williams' own work on forms and formations. For both men, elements within a social structure cannot be separated into a strictly causal hierarchy. Williams thought that it was arbitrary to isolate any singular element from within that totality and assign to it a strict causal primacy over all of the others.

[‡]   Jürgen Habermas from the Frankfurt School of Critical Theory and the last great European public intellectual.
[§]   Pierre Bourdieu was Professor of Sociology in Paris and a public intellectual

This led him to resist the distinction between base and superstructure, placing the emphasis instead on how a social order is constituted through a range of interrelated activities, all of which can be seen as being in some way material practices, but whose precise properties will be overlooked if they are merely reduced to the status of an economic base.

Before Williams' encounter with Goldmann, Louis Althusser had written of the need for a precise distinction between practices within a social totality. Dialectical relations are established by articulating distinct practices as they relate to one another, by 'thinking their degree of independence, their type of relative autonomy' (*Reading Capital*, p. 58). For Althusser too, social and material practices wield a degree of direct autonomous power, but in the last instance this power is always related back to one powerful system, Marx's base. The relative autonomy of a practice is in fact defined in Althusser's work by its 'type of dependence with respect to the type of practice which is determinant in the last instance: the economy.'

This is a position which Williams would crucially modify as his reading of continental critical theory deepened. Williams suggests that the economy is only causally effective because its power is manifested through a range of other social and material practices. In *The Long Revolution* he identifies four systems crucial to the development of social and cultural life. These are the system of decision; the system of maintenance; the system of learning and communication and the system of generation and nurture. Roughly speaking, by these systems Williams means politics, the economy, education and care for others. In capitalist society, all of the emphasis is placed upon the first two. He refers to this as a 'conditioned reflex to various forms of class society' in which 'the true nature of society – a human organization for common needs – was in fact filtered through the interests in power and property which were natural to ruling groups.' To acquiesce to this filtered view of society is to remain entrapped by the power of the economic base.

If we were able to reveal the extent to which this power can only operate by suppressing the systems of communication and generation, we would be able to rethink social determinism. In *Politics and Letters*, Williams refuses to see the industrial revolution solely as a transformation in economic relations:

> For the industrial revolution was among other things a revolution in the production of literacy and it is at this point that the argument turns full circle. The steam press was as much a part of the industrial revolution as the steam jenny or the steam locomotive. What it was producing was literacy, and with it a new kind of newspaper and novel. The traditional formulations that I was attacking would have seen the press as only a reflection at a much later stage of the economic order, which had produced the political order which had then produced the cultural order which had produced the press. Whereas the revolution itself, as a transformation of the mode of production, already included many changes which the ordinary definitions…

said were not economic. The task was not to see how the industrial revolution affected other sectors, but to see that it was an industrial revolution in the production of culture as much as an industrial revolution in clothing... or in the production of light, of power, of building materials.

The forces active at the economic base have no power in the abstract. They are only effective because they operate in and through systems of communication and nurture as well as through the systems of decision and maintenance. In Althusser's terms, these systems then retain a relative autonomy. There is thus no two-tiered structure of economic decision and superstructural reaction and effect. There is rather an integration of all social activities, mutually constituting and informing. The precise extent to which an economic, cultural or political practice exercises some determination over some kind of realised outcome will depend on the precise situation in question. Publishers, for example, reproduce the capitalist structure of society by subscribing to the profit imperative of the competitive economy. But publishers also operate as purveyors and contesters of ideology, an activity in which the economy is not the sole – or even the main – determinant. The practice of a fully integral cultural materialism neither denies the impact of economic causality nor assigns it a privileged status as sole determinant of cultural conditions. Williams' emphasis is on paying precise attention to actual practices, demonstrating situations in which the economy does play a greater or lesser role, and others in which other practices in education, government, cultural production and art might also play a determining role because these too are socially active material practices:

> The social and political order which maintains a capitalist market, like the social and political struggles which created it, is necessarily a material production. From castles and palaces and churches to prisons and workhouses and schools; from weapons of war to a controlled press: any ruling class, in variable ways though always materially, produces a social and political order. These are never superstructural activities. They are the necessarily material production within which an apparently self-subsistent mode of production can alone be carried on. The complexity of this process is especially remarkable in advanced capitalist societies, where it is wholly beside the point to isolate 'production' and 'industry' from the comparably material production of 'defence', 'law and order', 'welfare', 'entertainment' and 'public opinion'.

Williams' emphasis is on a social totality. Different processes are not collapsed into each other, but within the overall structure of society different practices cannot be considered in isolation since they mutually inform, constitute and at times contradict and conflict with each other. It is a social totality in which literature is not to be regarded as some kind of documentary record, produced after the event. Rather, the creation of literature participates in the creation of society and cannot therefore be seen as mere secondary reflection on it. There is an integrated social whole consisting of an interrelated body of material practices, mutually though varyingly informing each other. There is not a reified division between base economic activities on one hand and secondary superstructural symptoms on the other. Education, literature, industry, politics all relate to the same social totality, in ways which are mutually though unevenly informing.

It is not into society as an abstract that an individual is born, but into a range of social, political, cultural and economic relationships that comprise the society. In Williams' view language itself is one of these networks, and we will only understand its features if we take into account the active social relationships inside which it is used. Williams is aware that language use is not arbitrary, that the signs which we choose to use must carry some agreed meaning without which language could not operate as a system of communication. That is what he means when suggesting that words really do represent some genuine fusion of formal element with meaning. If words were altogether unhinged from this meaning communication would be impossible.

This chapter continues exploring how Williams related with contemporaries, by comparing two texts, *Drama From Ibsen to Eliot* from 1952 and 'The Importance of Community' in 1977, when cultural materialism showed signs of extended engagement with European writers across history, linguistics, sociology and associate fields.

In the introduction to *Drama From Ibsen to Eliot*, Williams sets out an early critical and methodological position. The approach is a textual one, concentrating on isolated individual works of drama. 'It is literary criticism also, which, in its major part is based on demonstrated judgements from texts, rather than on historical survey or generalised impressions.' The relation of cultural production to social processes is explicitly not his concern at this stage. In *Drama from Ibsen to Eliot*, his method is a literary-critical one, suggesting that the overall design of a dramatist is best realised when he or she retains direct control of the play. That is, high art requires strict policing:

> It seems to me that the most valuable drama is achieved when the technique of performance reserves to the dramatist primary control. It does not greatly matter whether this control is direct or indirect. In an age when it is accepted that the centre of drama is language, such control is reasonably assured. For when the centre of the drama is language, the *form* of the play will be essentially literary: the dramatist will adopt certain conventions of language through which to work. And if in such a case, the technique of performance – methods of speaking, movement and design – is of such a kind that it will communicate completely the conventions of the dramatist, the full power of the drama is available to be deployed.

Communication as an aesthetic experience is best achieved in Williams' view when an experience is expressed in such a way that it embodies the essence of the experience, while at the same time working that expression up into a new and intensified form, whose effect is to make the audience or receiver of the communication probe and question the meaning of the experience being conveyed. This to Williams is the basis of an aesthetic theory of communication: the irrefutable relation which exists between communicator and audience. The fact of communication cannot be understood as an active living process without taking into account these two poles of the process, interacting with each other. Communication is above all then the combination of expression and response. This would later form the dual focus of cultural materialism. The communicative nature of cultural materialism can be understood alongside the German rationalist Jürgen Habermas' notion of *communicative action*.

In his *Theory of Communicative Action*, Habermas makes a distinction between two different kinds of communication. The first of these conceives of communication as a one-way flow from communicator to receiver, where in the process of transferring whatever point he wishes to put across, the communicator simultaneously cancels out the fact of communication in some kind of fulfilled or realised action. This action is to the advantage or in the interest of the communicator and the unidirectional nature of this communication allows the communication which enables the fostering of such advantage to pass unquestioned. Habermas thus terms it *strategic* communication.

In the second type of communication suggested by Habermas' scheme, communication is oriented towards achieving understanding among two or more communicants, rather than towards the specific strategic advantage of one. Habermas believes this *understanding-directed* communication to depend on a concept of rationality whereby reason can only function if two or more communicants are able to express their feelings or emotions without keeping back any element of those feelings. To keep anything back would be to seek strategic advantage in the process of communication. When all ideas are put forward and examined, the implicit idea is that all of them will be modified by each other on the rational basis of the recognition of alternative claims to validity:

> We call an action oriented to success *strategic* when we consider it under the aspect of following rules of rational choice and assess the efficiency of influencing the decisions of a rational opponent. Instrumental actions can be connected with and subordinated to social interactions of a different type – for example as the 'task elements' of social roles; strategic actions are social actions by themselves. By contrast, I shall speak of *communicative action* whenever the actions of the agents involved are coordinated not through egocentric calculations of success but through acts of reaching understanding. In communicative action participants are not primarily oriented to their own individual successes; they pursue their individual goals under the condition that they can harmonize their plans of action on the basis of common situation definitions. In this respect, the negotiation of definitions of the situation is an essential element of the interpretive accomplishments required for communicative action.

Of the two kinds of communication Habermas proposes, the latter – communicative action – more exactly corresponds to Raymond Williams' idea of active communication via drama. For Williams conceives of drama as a form that cannot operate without a strong sense of its audience; cannot function as communication if the crucial fact of audience response is not taken to be an integral part of the process of communication where both the idea or experience being communicated and the ideas or experiences of the audience are mutually modified by their consideration of the other. Habermas' communicative action proposed to replace a communications rationale oriented towards the establishment of absolute truth, with the interaction of certain *validity claims,* regulated by their recognition – or otherwise – as social norms. He notes that in the process of communication,

> many arguments are not at all concerned with statements that one has to decide are 'true' of 'false', but with questions like, for example, what is good, what is beautiful, or what one ought to do. It is clear that we are here concerned more than ever with what is valid, with what is valid for certain people at certain times. The concept of prepositional truth is in fact too narrow to cover everything for which participants in argument claim validity in the logical sense. For this reason the theory of argumentation must be equipped with a more comprehensive concept of validity that is not restricted to the sense of validity in the sense of truth. But it does not at all follow from this that we

have to renounce concepts of validity analogous to truth,
to expunge every counterfactual moment from the concept
of validity and to equate validity with context-dependent
acceptability.

Habermas' validity claims do not offer to provide access
to an absolute truth. Instead, they ground their social util-
ity in the fact that they are capable of being modified and
extended as communication shifts from expression to
rational response. This is the same process of communication that Raymond Williams valued in successful cultural production. In other words, although Habermas is a
younger contemporary, his work informs and is informed
by Williams. There is thus not surprisingly a reciprocal relationship at work between cultural materialism as Williams
was developing it throughout his career, and other strands
of European critical theory.

If this kind of communication is to be achieved, the
challenge confronting the dramatist is how to express it
in an appropriate form, in short; it is a matter of dramatic
convention. Discussing August Strindberg's *The Father*,
Williams makes an important definition of convention.
Convention and *conventional* are not words which mean
merely ordinary and everyday as we often use them and
which implies direct naturalist representation. They imply
the conscious employment of theatrical devices which force
us to remember that we are watching a play, an illusion.
This lessens a tendency to look for reality in the sense of
plausibility or consistency and focus instead on the overall

dramatic theme as it is communicated through unity of speech with action.

Unfortunately in performance, the characters, as they are acted by real people, lose this quality of convention, so that they become just everyday figures, real people. Williams identifies this result in the course of performance to be deeply unconventional because the element of conscious theatricality is then lacking. He believes that in much twentieth-century theatre there is a total lack of this conscious use of theatrical convention, with the effect that the potentially transformative process of critical communication is removed because the emphasis is placed instead on an 'attempt to represent everyday speech'.

Jürgen Habermas invokes the *dramaturgical* as a mode of communication. His concept of the dramaturgical is not something restricted to the theatre, but a process of communication in the social world. It can usefully be applied to Williams' early work on drama because it allows us to see beginning there insights which had important implications for much broader social processes. Later, strands would be worked up in theorising the role literature plays in society. *Dramaturgical communication* refers

> primarily neither to the solitary actor, nor to members of a social group, but to participants in interaction constituting a public for one another, before whom they present themselves. The actor evokes in his public a certain image, an impression of himself, by more or less purposefully disclosing his subjectivity. Each agent can monitor public

access to the system of his own intentions, thoughts, attitudes, desires, feelings and the like, to which only he has privileged access. In dramaturgical action, participants make use of this and steer their interactions through regulating mutual access to their own subjectivities. Thus the central concept of *presentation of self* does not signify spontaneous expressive behaviour but stylising one's own experiences with a view to the audience.

Stylising one's own experience with regard to the audience could be a definition of Williams' concept of *convention* in drama. A rational communicative action oriented towards achieving understanding between subjects rather than the strategic advantage of one, requires that in the process of communication, nothing be held back. But at the same time, the process of communicating information will inevitably be selective.

Habermas therefore suggests that dramaturgical action often does not contribute to the process of understanding-oriented communication he outlines. The dramaturgical, he suggests, often degenerates into a mode of communication where one party is seeking strategic advantage over another, and this clearly obstructs the understanding-oriented communication which both he and Williams value. When this is applied to drama as such, a serious connective art is impeded.

Williams believed that communication is best achieved as a process when the artist, dramatist, writer or communicator in question finds the forms and conventions which are most appropriate to the experience he is seeking to convey while still being recognisable to the audience as conventions of communication rather than as an end in themselves. This essential tension between the familiar and the innovative is what provides the intensified feeling that enables artistic production to function as a profound source of communication. That the concept of communication is not confined merely to drama but applies to social processes more generally is evident in Habermas' conclusion that norm-based validity claims – which I have suggested are equivalent to Williams' conventions – can be criticised and modified

> in any number of ways – by handing over information, raising a legal claim, raising objections to the adoption of a new strategy (e.g., a business policy) or a new technique (e.g., in the slalom or in steel production), by criticizing a musical performance, defending a scientific hypothesis, supporting a candidate in competition for a job, and so forth. What is common to these cases is the form of argumentation: We try to support a claim with good grounds or reasons; the quality of the reasons or their relevance can be called into question by the other side; we meet objections and are forced in some cases to modify our original position.

Raymond Williams' appraisal of drama can be considered paradigmatic of a cultural materialist conception of communication more broadly, precisely because the same arguments obtain in such radically different spheres of social life. The common thread is the emphasis in each case on communication as a social process rather than a strategic instrument.

The dramatisation of consciousness is an important theme in his lecture at a Plaid Cymru conference in 1977, 'The Importance of Community', where Williams asserts the need to combine cultural analysis with contemporary political intervention. The greatest obstacle to progress was the extent to which governing ideas had become entrenched within individual minds, thus foreclosing in advance the possibility of envisaging alternatives:

> This was my saddest discovery: when I found that in myself – and of course by this time I had been away and through a very different experience – in myself that most crucial form of imperialism had happened. That is to say, where parts of your mind are taken over by a system of ideas, a system of feelings, which really do emanate from the power centre. Right back in your own mind, and right back inside the oppressed and deprived community, there are reproduced elements of the thinking and the feeling of that dominating centre.

Between the work on drama in 1952 and this later essay in 1977, a shift had taken place in Williams' thinking. Williams' reference to being away through a very different experience, was acknowledgement of prolonged absence from Wales, to which return in the late sixties enhanced awareness of European connections. The movement from a working-class community in Wales to Cambridge and a middle-class profession, had meant working within the dominant formation for much longer than he could have expected. Recognising that experience registered as a shock to Williams, inviting him to re-examine his own Welshness, and recognise affiliation with a European tradition as an alternative to the dominant culture of the English middle class against which he reacted to achieve critical distance.

In 1952, the dramatisation of consciousness had been a weapon of empowerment, the means of communicating a direct experience embodied in a perfectly integrated and conventional dramatic form, with the potential to suggest a socially transformative critical naturalism. By 1977, however, the dramatisation of consciousness has become identified by Williams as an antithetical process: a tie-in between the ruling political formations of the day and the private commercial institutions of broadcasting who manufacture a perpetual flow of images that will actually govern how we live, shaped according to the political or economic expedients of an elite.

In *The Theory of Communicative Action*, Jürgen Habermas shows that real communication can only be achieved in a situation where nothing is excluded, kept back from the communication process. Failure to engage with the majority of the population in effect blocks any truly social communication at all. 'The failure is due to an arrogant preoccupation with transmission, which rests on the assumption that the common answers have been found and need only be applied.'

The early idea that communication is best achieved when the artist and his or her audience share a body of values and experiences can be identified with a narrow elitism which Williams failed to acknowledge earlier, whereas the later definition retains a sense of the importance of common experiences. By then the emphasis has shifted to suggest that these common elements are only really unleashed in communicative action when the different elements and experiences comprising a whole culture are brought into relation with each other, rather than merely extending or imposing one element on another. By comparison to the early work, the later position is hugely sophisticated.

By the time *Drama From Ibsen to Eliot* had been rewritten as *Drama From Ibsen to Brecht* in 1968, a number of key changes had taken placed in Williams' thinking as his cultural theory deepened. The emphasis was now very much more on an integrated social totality, in which different cultural forms circulate and inform the very structures underpinning society. Revisions indicate important developments in Williams' materialism of culture: the relation between forms and formations; the modification of the idea of base and superstructure; and the materiality of language itself. The key change is that the exercise is now less overtly a practical-critical one in the way the introduction to the earlier work had proclaimed: the analysis is now prepared to embrace the questions of context, history and society which were either downplayed or left vague and abstract in the earlier work.

Jürgen Habermas' idea of argumentation is based on

an idea of validity claims, rather than on the notion of an anterior absolute truth which the process of communication could simply establish without complication. At the same time, Habermas refuses to renounce a concept of validity that is analogous to truth precisely in the sense that the norms by which validity claims may be disputed or regulated are felt as absolute even while they remain partial constructs. Habermas refuses to give way either to a relativising of cultural structures or to a cultural absolutism:

> But if the validity of arguments can be neither undermined in an empiricist manner nor grounded in an absolutist manner, then we are faced with precisely those questions to which the logic of argumentation is supposed to provide the answers: How can problematic validity claims be supported by good reasons? How can reasons be criticized in turn? What makes some arguments, and thus some reasons, which are related to validity claims in a certain way, stronger or weaker than other arguments?

Williams proposes to probe the tension between partial constructions and their experience as absolutes by looking at precisely these traces, for these are what give him access to the structure of feeling.

The real tension is again between an apparent causality or determinism, and the registering of the potential for change which is profoundly anti-deterministic. This bears more generally on how different elements within a social whole can play an active role in the creation of material conditions of social being, and at certain moments of historical conjunction each individual element can take on a temporarily causal and deterministic primacy.

In 1971 Williams gave a lecture in memory of Lucien Goldmann. The two men had only recently come to exchange ideas in person rather than through print, when the dialogue was cut short by the other's sudden death. Now speaking of that loss and the importance of Goldmann, Williams looked back on his own work. He recalls how from *Culture and Society* and on through *The Long Revolution*, he had been writing in relative isolation, and the work of figures such as Goldmann as yet unknown. It is a disclosure that makes Williams' status as a genuinely original thinker, to which perhaps the word genius might wisely be restricted, all the more apparent. Summarising this effort, Williams goes on to describe how he had been trying

> to see the study of culture as the study of relations between elements in a whole way of life; to find ways of studying structure in particular works and periods, which could stay in touch with and illuminate particular art-works and forms, but also forms and relations of more general social life; to replace the formula of base and superstructure with the more active idea of a field of mutually if also unevenly determining forces.

The question then becomes one of what historical forces need to be brought into conjunction with each other in such a way as to afford one element of the social totality a momentary causal efficacy over the others in the same field of elements. To address this issue, the concept Williams later developed is that of formation: not now simply the question of how things are put together to create a view of the world, but how these things are socially, historically, institutionally and technologically aligned. Once we grasp this, we are better able to apprehend the possibility for intervention and change.

A good example of this can be seen in his analysis in the 1968 book of Strindberg's *Road to Damascus*. Williams argues that the play was in a tangible way a prefiguring of the later technologies of film, since it is a kind of writing which depends on dramatic conventions which are not yet technically available. Character is abandoned in favour of the creation of a 'total flow' of language communicating an experience by exerting control over the dramatic action, which is a manifestation of the experience being communicated.

In significant ways Williams argues the work of Ibsen and Strindberg pre-empted the cultural forms of television drama, so that we should not assume innovation in the latter was solely the result of technical change. Since he relates the drama directly to television culture, it is perhaps not surprising to find him using the same term – *flow* – for both. There is, in a manner of speaking, a progression in his integration of ideas, and conversely, his ideas of integration. The use of similar terms to enable critique in such apparently different spheres as nineteenth-century drama and twentieth-century media culture shows that this development was not a piecemeal one and this interrelation is the essence of cultural materialism.

A stress on interrelations between features of a society and across time enables a more dynamic sense of process expressed using the vocabulary of dominant, residual and emergent. A *dominant* ideology in a society is related to the ruling hegemony, tied in to large-scale institutions of broadcasting and cultural production and the images of society that these institutions implicitly reproduce. The current cultural dominant, Williams suggests, is a kind of mobile privatisation. That is, the combination of a worldview which values privacy and posits the individual as sovereign in all matters – individual expression, individual choice, individual consumption – with an unprecedented level of physical and cultural mobility.

The *residual* means not only the archaic but refers to those elements of the dominant which have become less visibly active in the daily life of a society, while at the same time retaining a strong latent power of their own. Examples Williams gives of the residual are rural communities, the established church and the monarchy. It is only *emergent* practices which can operate as truly oppositional forms, able to contest social and political processes. The emergence in the nineteenth century of the radical popular press is an important example.

In general, the residual elements of cultural formations have become incorporated to the dominant cultural mode of a society. The monarchy and the Church of England remain essential components of the British establishment although they are no longer the primary means by which political activity is carried out. The ongoing existence of powerful institutions underlines a very important point: that the tendency of the dominant cultural formation is always to incorporate external elements to itself so as to retain cultural dominance. *Incorporation* is important, for it is this which has most often to be resisted.

If the dominant cultural forms of a society attempt to achieve incorporation at every level of human practice, resistance can only be registered explicitly through conflict. It is the *residual not incorporated* elements of a social formation and their manifestation in singular cultural forms that for Williams provide the scope for intervention in the field of cultural production. We might think of his valuation of the epic theatre of Brecht, or the television work of Dennis Potter as examples. Cultural production then becomes a particularly powerful and specialist means of expressing and altering collectively held beliefs, their extension or modification. But Williams' work on language also reveals that art wields a certain power to elude the concept of purposive-rational communication altogether. Habermas' distinction between strategic goal-oriented communication and communication oriented towards achieving understanding is again relevant. For art to operate as a successful process of communication, Williams believes that the individual artist must express simultaneously his own values and those of the wider society around him. That is not to suggest that all the members of the society share identical experiences, beliefs and values. It suggests that an individual's values are simply one version, one selection, of the available meanings and values circulating within a society and which are therefore amenable to common expression without dictating a strict homogeneity of feeling to its members. The common elements in the society are not centrally determining but are de-centred, available to be moulded together in varying forms of expression.

If an individual's values constitute a selection of the general values, there is then a question of how this selection occurs. Williams, like French sociologist Pierre Bourdieu, believes that the individual form of a work of art is the product of forces acting simultaneously in the wider society, and in and through the individual artist. In Bourdieu's *The Field of Cultural Production,* this relation between individual artist and social forces is cast in terms of the two-level conflict over consecration in which cultural producers are not only – are not even primarily – the individual artists, but the whole network of relational figures:

> The incessant explication and redefinition of the foundations of his work provoked by criticism or the work of others determines a decisive transformation of the relation between the producer and his work, which reacts, in turn, on the work itself.

The co-existence of the intention of the individual artist's meaning with a de-centred but nevertheless widely circulating body of general meanings expresses the basis of what Williams terms the *emergent*. For if the individual meanings are merely one selection of the common and generally circulating values, the question becomes one of how this selection is made; where selection refers both to the act of making a deliberate, conscious choice and to the pre-existing set of categories from which that choice is made. The practice of cultural materialism should properly be understood as a dialogue, a double movement between individual innovation and critical engagement that precisely describes Williams the Welsh European and participant in an exchange of critical theory.

Raymond Williams

Drama from Ibsen to Eliot, Chatto and Windus, 1952.

Culture and Society, 1958, Spokesman, 2013.

The Long Revolution, 1961, Parthian, 2011.

Drama from Ibsen to Brecht, Chatto and Windus, 1968.

Marxism and Literature, Oxford University Press, 1977.

Politics and Letters, 1979, Verso, 2015.

Problems in Materialism and Culture, 1980, republished as *Culture and Materialism*, Verso radical thinkers, 2010.

Resources of Hope, edited Robin Gable, Verso, 1989.

Other works

Louis Althusser, *Reading Capital*, New Left Books, 1970.

Pierre Bourdieu, *The Field of Cultural Production*, Polity, 1993.

Hywel Dix, *After Raymond Williams*, 2008, UWP, 2013.

Jürgen Habermas, *Theory of Communicative Action Volume One: Reason and the Rationalization of Society*, Heinemann, 1983.

Lucien Goldmann, *The Hidden God*, 1964, Verso, 2016

8

Sowing the Seeds of Change

Hywel Dix

Two key elements in the genesis of Raymond Williams' critical thinking were his Welsh nationality, and his constant concern for bringing sociological and political insights to questions of culture. These factors aligned Williams and his work with a greater number of European thinkers than a summary survey of his published work might suggest. In this sense it may be that Williams was at his most Welsh when he was simultaneously at his most European, and conversely, as he told the *Politics and Letters* interviewers:

> Through the intricacies of the politics, and they are very intricate indeed, I want the Welsh people – still a very radical and cultured people – to defeat, override or bypass bourgeois England; the alternatives follow from the intricacies. That connects, for me, with the sense in my work that I am now necessarily European; that

the people to the left and on the left of the French and
Italian communist parties, the German and Scandinavian
comrades, the communist dissidents from the East like
Bahro, are my kind of people; the people I come from and
belong to, and my more conscious Welshness is, as I feel
it, my way of learning those connections.

Williams was not known for referring to his contemporaries directly in print and it is characteristic of his meth-
odology that in this famous passage where he identified
himself as a Welsh European, he refers to only one other
individual European thinker by name. Rudolf Bahro's *The
Alternative in Eastern Europe* had been published in German
in 1977, and by Verso in English translation in 1978, just a
year before Williams' *Politics and Letters*. If we add to the mix
that between 1970 and 1976 Tom Nairn published a series
of articles, that in 1977 became more widely available in his
influential *The Break-Up of Britain*, we sense that this was
an important period for Williams' distinctive thinking on
nation, state and politics – thinking that in the subsequent
years of political devolution across the United Kingdom
has become increasingly pertinent.

This chapter explores Bahro's *Alternative in Eastern
Europe* as a significant contribution to events that brought
together questions of the British state and ways of thinking
about democracy, and which remain integral to struggles for
political representation in the twenty-first century. More
specifically, the chapter examines connections between
Bahro's work and Raymond Williams', and in particular

his talk 'Are We Becoming More Divided?' prepared for television somewhere between 1973 and 1976, and a later Socialist Society publication 'Democracy and Parliament' that appeared in 1982, where ideas began in the earlier text are extended. 'Are We Becoming More Divided?' was published in *Radical Wales* in 1989, and both essays have much to say on the ongoing contest for effective forms of political democracy in a partially devolved Britain.

Rudolf Bahro wrote *The Alternative in Eastern Europe* over a period of four years from 1973 to 1976, coinciding with the successful revolution in Portugal and when the revolutionary upheavals of 1968 were very much in his mind. One of his starting points in *The Alternative in Eastern Europe* was the fact that the events of 1968 in Western Europe and of the same year in the so-called Communist bloc had been presented as qualitatively different kinds of experience. But what, Bahro wondered, if there were connections between the quashing of student rebellion in France and suppression of the Prague Spring in Czechoslovakia followed by defeat in 1970 of the Polish dockers' attempts at political freedom? 'What is the significance of the defeats of the West European revolutionary movement, from 1918 in Germany through to 1968 in France? There must be a connection in all this, to illuminate the present scene.'

Bahro's 'present scene' has a very precise meaning. Polish Commentator Jan Kott had appropriated Shakespeare for an eastern European readership in a landmark study entitled *Shakespeare: Our Contemporary*. Kott argued that the atmosphere of secrecy, distrust, plotting, spying and revenge that pervades Shakespearean tragedy was exactly replicated in the system of divide and rule that existed in the eastern European societies under dictatorship during the seventies and that this made Shakespearean drama alive to such a society in a way that was impossible in the west. When Kott uses the words 'our contemporary' the 'our' in question refers specifically to the people in those societies at that time. Bahro's *Alternative* is similarly littered with constant references to 'we', 'us' and 'our situation' and it must be understood that the 'we' he uses refers specifically to dissident intellectuals in eastern Europe during the sixties and seventies. In other words, his 'present scene' is the political settlement of that society, and when he sets out to explore how the defeat of political dissidence in Western European countries is related to it, what he is specifically attempting to theorise is the connection that exists between the political order of the capitalist West and the travesty of Communist principles in the East. Bahro's eastern European dissidents were people to whom 'Communist' was a point of reference to which they could affirm, but for who, as Raymond Williams put it, the *idea* of socialism has been confiscated by the ruling hierarchies.

It would be simplistic to see *The Alternative in Eastern Europe* as presenting a straightforward option between the dictatorship of communism and the assumed freedom of the capitalist West, indeed Bahro's commitment makes such a dichotomy impossible. Again and again he makes a distinction between communism as an aspiration toward human emancipation, and its travesty in the guise of 'actually existing socialism'. Indeed, there is a sense of pride in his work that eastern Europe, as against the capitalist West, had managed to retain a commitment to communist ideals despite the actual history. He refers to this travesty as 'tragedy' in exactly the same way that Williams had earlier referred to certain political defeats as *tragic* in *Modern Tragedy*. Instead of a series of compromised options between a system of welfare democracy and socialist dictatorship he explores the genesis of industrial society in both spheres and explores ways in which each might be in need of reform so that rather than a straight alternative between the systems of east and west there is a further alternative that relates to the connections between both and their common movement towards human emancipation.

Bahro's analysis of the genealogy of industrial society is rooted in a detailed reading of the work of Marx. Bahro was particularly struck by the assertion that it is the bourgeoisie themselves who create the material conditions necessary for revolution. Having appropriated the means of production for themselves, the bourgeoisie must then be overthrown, abolishing private property by creating common ownership of the material elements of society and hence creating social capital controlled by – or on behalf of – the people. The gap that occurs between these stages, that is, between the overthrow of the bourgeois and the creation of a properly social stock of capital characterises eastern Europe under the control of a one-party dictatorship. This to Bahro is the tragedy of the revolution. Again, however, Bahro emphasises the 'us-ness' of his own society, the distinct nature of the society whose genesis he sought to understand theoretically. He suggests that the abolition of private property is not necessarily a prerequisite for revolutionary socialism in all societies because not all societies have been historically based on concepts of private ownership. Bahro suggests that the USSR should not be understood according to a European model of economic and industrial development, but rather as an Asiatic Society, characterised by economic despotism in the same way that societies of the Incas, Egyptians or Chinese were despotic, but where there was an underlying sense that all land and hence capital belonged to the societies themselves. Property in the economic despotism of Asiatic societies was 'managed' by a priestly or administrative class on behalf of the whole society, creating a quite different social contract from that of European monarchy or aristocracy where individual private ownership is paramount.

The concept of a managerial or bureaucratic class is of central relevance to how Bahro understands the tragedy of eastern Europe and the alternative possibilities of democracy in both east and west. For example, he suggests that to achieve revolution in Russia in 1917, it was necessary to develop the nation's industrial capability and so create the conditions for material equality. When it came, the development of industry did not mean that the millions of industrial workers had any political or military power. Authority and decision-making processes were managed on their behalf in the industrial and economic despotism of Stalin – not founded on private property like agrarian capitalism but pursuing the alternative logic of Lenin's New Economic Policy.

Bahro describes the trajectory of Soviet history as the 'non-capitalist road to industrial development' because it amounts to an attempt to catch up with some of the societies in western Europe in material terms, but with different economic and political structures. The industrialisation of the USSR occurred in a 'belated' manner, coming *after* the change of social structures brought about by the revolution but lacking the social organisation of Britain and France. The Soviet trajectory has for Bahro a special status as an example of how non-capitalist societies seek to catch up with the west through material industrialisation and develop a nascent bureaucratic or managerial structure in order to handle the process, with the result that revolution becomes folded back into dictatorship. The rule by a managerial class over the people is how Bahro thinks eastern European societies throughout the seventies could be characterised, and it is a process in which the state performs an important multiple role.

If truly social capital were to be created, Bahro suggests, the division of labour must be overcome. While it exists, social equality is hindered by sharp differences of living pattern between men and women, between workers engaged in qualitatively different work, and perhaps most significantly between those with access to higher or lower levels of education. Those who receive the lowest level of education, in particular, have no access to a critical cultural or political reflection and as a result can have no involvement in the processes of decision making and planning. 'The organizational mastery on the basis of the division of labour is from the very beginning a problem of a structure of consciousness which appears as a relationship between people.' The dominant relationship that Bahro detected under actually existing socialism in the seventies was not one of different social classes, as in capitalist societies. But neither was it a horizontal axis based on comradeship and equality. Instead, it was a hierarchy of functions based on different capacities to perform specific functions in the state as a whole. How had this come about?

The *plan* is a central element in Rudolf Bahro's analysis of the economic totalitarianism of actually existing socialism in the seventies. His use of the term has perhaps two purposes; first, he wished to make a distinction between two different orientations in industrial society – the orientation of the market, and the orientation of a party bureaucratic structure. Second, he wished to draw attention to the inhuman element of the managerial dictatorship of actually existing socialism, and its tendency to neglect human social and psychological needs. The plan, in Bahro's terms, is inflexible, abstract and inhuman, promoting mediocrity and drudgery without paying attention to the physical, emotional or cultural needs of those who carry it out. 'The result is that the productive and creative elements suffer from an increase in mediocrity, indeed incompetence, dishonourable behaviour and insecurity in official positions, not to speak here of the political standardization that is required.' The plan blandly flattens individual needs and reduces them to the needs of its own existence. This is a travesty of Lenin's ideal model, which proposed the idea of a relationship between 'party/ trade union/ masses' as a 'transmission mechanism' whereby executive decision would be vested in the communist party on behalf of the people with the trade unions serving an intermediary function, supposedly guaranteeing a position for the people in the party and hence in the decision-making processes of the state.

However, the structure of bureaucratic dictatorship is one of entrapment. Whereas the idea behind capitalist societies is advancement on merit, the social stratification created by such a structure was one of little or no mobility and little or no access to systems of information or critical literacy. To Bahro, defeat of new revolutionary impulses in 1968 was symptomatic of a managerial compromise that is essentially bourgeois and corporate in nature. For this reason, Bahro's concept of the *plan* has a much wider application than the society in which it was applied. Bahro attributed the quelling of dissident agitation in eastern Europe and the defeat of student political unrest in the west equally to the material compromises of the managerial plan. Moreover, he warned that if the then nascent European Economic Community was to become more of a super-state, 'without regenerating itself in some neo-proletarian manner', then a further tightening of the grip of an inhuman managerial structure on political power could be expected. In other words, the alternative in eastern Europe is not a choice between economic systems but a question of whether or not a new system could be found that opened beyond each.

Bahro's work, apparently so rooted in the conditions of a particular place, time and political system, turns out to provide important insight into a wider whole. Bahro was interested in how to open up new forms of democracy in both east and west. Thus it is no surprise that his work finds a direct counterpart in that of Raymond Williams in the west.

In *Towards 2000*, Williams sets out his thinking on the genesis of welfare democracy in Britain, the capitalist compromise, the crises of the seventies and a series of potential futures for British societies. Like Bahro, he explores a series of alternative political decisions that depart from a simple dichotomy between capitalism and socialism, that is, beyond party politics, and attempts to theorise a more fundamental series of choices that will impact directly upon the nature of British society for generations to come.

In the concluding section entitled 'Resources for a Journey of Hope' Williams outlines one potential future, that he labels *Plan X*:

It is indeed a plan, as distinct from the unthinking reproduction of distraction. But it is different from other kinds of planning, and from all other ways of thinking about the future, in that its objective is indeed 'X': a willed and deliberate unknown, in which the only defining factor is advantage... [W]hat is new in 'Plan X' politics is that it has genuinely incorporated a reading of the future, and one which is quite deeply as pessimistic, in general terms, as the most extreme readings of those who are now campaigning against the nuclear arms race or the extending damage of the ecological crisis.

Rudolf Bahro's use of the term *plan* identifies a principle of governance in the abstract, a condition of permanent power. The same is true of Williams' Plan X; it has no orientation, but rather is a critical perception of a potential economic and political condition in which exists a loop between the exercise of power and maintaining advantage. As such Bahro and Williams both identify a situation where rule travesties the very principle of common interest in whose name it purports to speak.

Again and again in the work of both Williams and Bahro, access to the structures of political and economic planning is invoked as the single most necessary element of a newly democratised society. This brings in its train implications about the importance of the educational franchise and the role of a critical consciousness-raising education, away from a mere functional literacy and embracing a fuller cultural and political awareness. Input into the processes of decision making and planning by the majority is needed for social emancipation to occur and for the societies in question to be democratised while retaining at least an element of the original ideals of their architects. To create the framework capable of bringing this about, both writers are aware, would be tantamount to a cultural revolution.

The final section of Bahro's *Alternative in Eastern Europe* is devoted to sketching out a series of proposals for democratising the political structures of contemporary eastern European society. The four specific proposals that he expounds are the establishment of a new scrutiny body to root out and liquidate political corruption in all its forms; the abolition of imposed patterns of labour for workers in radically different fields of endeavour; the 'planned periodic participation of the entire managerial and intellectual staff of society in simple operative labour'; and a revised system of wage scales that will not reflect an individual's level of education but will be more anchored in a principle of equality. There appears to be some confusion in Bahro's thinking on these matters: the proposal to abolish the concept of piecemeal work seems to be an acknowledgement that even in eastern Europe by the seventies, not all productive work could be characterised as industrial labour, and that a whole range of non-comparable and non-corresponding functions existed within the non-capitalist economy. At the same time, the fourth proposal appears to contradict such an acknowledgement completely, cancelling the differences between different kinds of productive work and ushering in a concept of equal pay for equal hours – regardless of the work that is discharged in those hours.

On surer ground perhaps, Bahro concludes the *Alternative* with five further proposals in the area of cultural politics: individual consciousness and the development of individual expression as themselves having to be materially produced and hence enriching rather than diverting from the overall stock of social capital; a new way of approaching human needs that would transcend the traditional emphasis on raw materials which arguably provokes competition and aggression in pursuit of those things; a corresponding shift in attitudes to material production that would incorporate some sense of common ownership and re-use of resources even after they have been expended; a new economy of time that is not harnessed directly to the planned or to the market; and perhaps most significantly, what Bahro refers to as 'structural conditions of individual initiative and genuine commonality: society as an association of communes.'

It is worth dwelling on this final point for some time. The association of communes that Bahro adumbrates is his strongest proposal and the one that dominates the conclusion of *The Alternative in Eastern Europe*. It is also one of his strongest legacies for our own period. All over Europe, countries have increasingly embraced political structures far removed from the all-purpose units of an earlier era and have adopted a series of forms of representation that range in size and reach from local systems of decision to much larger-scale entities. In Britain, this is very apparent in the recent complications over devolution politics in Northern Ireland, Scotland and Wales, and latently apparent in a much more general trend towards reorganising local government. Reading Raymond Williams on specific and varying organs of political representation in *Towards 2000* together with Rudolf Bahro's *Alternative* can illuminate these matters and clarify the thinking of each of these difficult writers.

To Bahro, the question of the individual's relationship to the state is first and foremost a question of ideology. The state apparatus of actually existing socialism had developed as an organ of the need for belated industrialisation to create the material conditions for social equality. In a parallel movement, the party apparatus had evolved to fill the power vacuum created by the revolutionary movements of the post-1917 era. In theory, the party apparatus existed to act as an intermediary body between the people, the trade unions, and the political state – guaranteeing a certain level of consideration be given to the ideas and wishes of the unions in the process of political decision. In practice, the party apparatus functioned not so much as an intermediary but more as a buffer, cutting the people off from access to the very systems of decision it was designed to safeguard. The relationship between party, individual and state is ideological in the sense that the task of finding alternative means for expressing popular opinion, devolved on dissident intellectuals:

> The cultural revolution can in no way be conceived of as the action of a party and state bureaucracy, even one three times as 'enlightened' as the present. The apparatus does not think, it repeats what its founders programmed into it and what circumstances have since required of it in the way of superficial adaptive reactions. The idea and strategy of a social transformation cannot even be meaningfully discussed, let alone carried through, with people who have chiefly to consider what their superiors and colleagues will say about them.

Bahro refers to the first challenge to the party apparatus as a challenge of 'surplus consciousness'. This appears to refer to the capacity of the individual and any group or body outside the state or party apparatus to develop new forms of thinking and new means of political expression. It recognises *contra* certain dogmas of Bahro's own period that mental and creative work are as creative as industrial labour – they too can create a surplus capable of being trans-valued over and beyond their own inherent value. It gives rise to the question of how surplus consciousness is to be created and what is to be done with it.

It is important to remember Bahro and Williams' distinction between socialism as it was being lived in the totalitarian states of the s and communism as a concept. *Communist* political structures remained to Bahro the goal of an ongoing dissident politics. He used the term *socialist* to refer to the travestying of those ideals by existing material forces. This distinction is important because in the west, the two terms have tended to be used almost exactly the other way around. *Communism*, the goal of much of Bahro's work, is freighted with historical and political overdetermination so that in the west it has been hard to use it creatively, and indeed *communalism* might be a more accurate English word for the ideas that Bahro and Williams expressed.

In Bahro's context, communalism is neither an organised political system, nor a formally elaborated theoretical creed; although it is notable that it was both of these things simultaneously in the French commune of the 1870s, which features prominently in Bahro's writing precisely because it neither required its adherents to choose one concept over another. The Communards were an informal association of different interests, and this is the very idea behind much of Bahro's own theoretical research. The alternative that he propounds is not so much a choice between one party and another, or one political creed over another. It is a whole alternative system on the informal encounter between different interest groups dialogically. As a result, Bahro suggests that the best hope for representing multiple interest groups simultaneously is to cease thinking of one's relationship to the state through a particular party and think of it instead as an informal arrangement outside party lines. 'The factual existence of surplus consciousness – the potential for a League of Communists to replace the former party, and for its social sounding board, is no longer a mere hypothesis, and since 1968 we can see the practical possibility of establishing it.'

In Britain in the second decade of the twenty-first century it might seem difficult to conceive of a League of Communists able to create conditions for genuine social equality. If, however, we substitute for 'League of Communists' the idea of a 'League of Communalists' we will sense that Bahro is proposing a system whereby different political formations, together or independently, are enabled to carry out research, education and planning, so that instead of the ideology of the party, a surplus consciousness would emerge based on common needs and interests. A League of Communalists would enable not only industrial workers, feminists, carers, older people, children etc., to work together on mutual political education, policy formation and future planning in a way that would free them from obeisance either to one particular party or one particular cause. 'If the League of Communists is to be in this way the organ for the socialization of political unity and power of decision, then the first condition for this is a party constitution that is open towards all genuine social forces, which makes it possible to invite for collaboration and attract to it without any kind of exclusive sectarianism and power-secrecy behind closed doors, all the living and productive elements of labour and culture.'

Bahro's proposal of a League of Communists tends towards recognition of multiple different kinds of political and non-governmental organisations that exist, the specific issues that affect each and which in turn they seek to influence. Many of these – ecology, environmentalism, migration, nuclear disarmament – are by their very nature global issues and global movements that cannot be restricted by local policies even at the level of the nation-state. The governing principle of the proposal of the League of Communists is that all of these different kinds of body should be empowered to work together to shape and develop common policy to the general good.

A transnational league of Communalists would offer to provide equal access to a system of decision freed from the monotheistic state apparatus in any one country. Whereas a narrow selection of one political party over another restricts choice and so tends towards the bureaucratic dictatorship of a centralised state apparatus, a League of Communists would provide a form of 'collective sovereignty' that would uncouple the Party from the political state and generate a situation of 'dual supremacy in which the étatist side gradually becomes less dominant' and where the people, or at least, their freely chosen representatives, are genuinely able to take control of the systems of the decision that will shape their own lives. As Raymond Williams was aware, this is as true at the most local level as it is at the level of the nation-state and transnational organs of co-operation. There is an implication in Bahro's work that the gradual lessening of the federal principle in favour of local governmental power in nations across Europe is contradicted by the simultaneous agglomeration of those very levels into even larger, transnational political units. The contradiction can seem like less of a dilemma and more of a creative dynamic if we approach Bahro's work through the lens of Williams' reading of it.

The importance of Bahro's proposal for replacing single-purpose political parties with practical and affective variable units is discernible in Raymond Williams writing. 'Are We Becoming More Divided?' is a talk written in the mid-seventies, that sets the drive for devolution in Scotland and Wales in the context of two contrasting forms of nationalism. The 1982 essays 'Democracy and Parliament,' reprinted in *Towards 2000* and *Resources of Hope* picks up where 'Are We Becoming More Divided?' leaves off, expanding the scope of the discussion so that alternative political movements in Scotland and Wales are viewed alongside a renewed interest in the role and definition of local government at a range of levels and forms across Britain. What is taken forward here, however, is the potential that ideas for new variable units of political representation put forward in the two essays are tantamount to Bahro's *League of Communists*.

One of the important contributions that Williams makes to British democracy in 'Are we becoming more divided?' is to bring the term *Devolution* into the open and give it a clear sense of definition: 'One of the first things people think of when it is said, sadly, that we are becoming more divided, is the growth of nationalist movements in Scotland and Wales: a growth that has led to arguments about what is called devolution.' As often in Williams' work, the irony of the word 'sadly' comes as a pointed clue as to what is to follow. It soon becomes clear that to Williams, the onset of alternative nationalisms in Scotland and Wales, and the implied loss of unity at Britain's political centre, is a development neither to be lamented nor fully embraced: 'But it depends where you are, where you are seeing this growth from.'

'Growth' is entirely the correct word for a number of reasons. Firstly, it is a verb of subtly ambiguous status. It is a transitive verb, a verb requiring an object, a verb referring to an action that cannot simply occur but has to be made actively to occur by an outside agent. Secondly and at the same time, it can also be read as an intransitive verb, a verb with no agent, a verb describing an action that really does cause itself to happen. The interplay between these two different nuances of the verb perhaps expresses some of the history of political devolution in Scotland and Wales during the period in question: a growth both hastened into reality by the active intervention of others and actively hastening the work of others in its turn. Devolution in this sense was both grown by those modern Celtic radicals who worked for it, and a wider historical development transcending the intervention of individuals. If devolution had not existed because of the work of its proponents, we might say, it would have been necessary to invent it because of the drive of history.

Thirdly, the term *growth* has important implications for a process in continual development, rather than a singular event that occurs once and can then be taken for granted forever. Indeed, the process of devolution is one that continued to unfold in the years between Williams' contribution to the campaign for political devolution in 1977–79, his death in 1988, the referenda of 1997 which reversed the results of 18 years before, and in the years that have followed the first sessions of the Scottish Parliament and the then Welsh Assembly, now Senedd or Welsh Parliament. These different historical moments are enough to show that the process remains as alive, ongoing and contested in the twenty-first century as it was in 1977, and that any attempt to draw attention to the evolving complexities of the questions involved are still as important as they were.

The emphasis on evolving complexities is the contribution that Williams makes to political democracy in 'Are We Becoming More Divided?' He was aware that there was no simple model for political devolution in Scotland or Wales and that as such any development would have to be carefully attuned to the nuances of the time. In his novel *The Volunteers*, published during the same period, he had portrayed a then-futuristic world in which home rule for Scotland and Wales had been 'granted' from an alien Westminster administration as a kind of minimal concession, denying any real self-determination to the peoples of the nations in question while also offering to forestall the demand for thoroughgoing change. As he would later note in 'Democracy and Parliament',

> it is then a matter of great urgency to distinguish between this now active and hopeful movement, between the genuine democratic impulses which are intended to improve and extend parliamentary democracy, and the actual methods proposed, which in their existing form – without shorter parliaments, without proportional representation, without reforms of Conference, without primary democratic selection of all delegates and candidates, without procedures of positive recall, and unicameral could go as easily in the direction of a command-bureaucratic government as in the direction of socialist democracy.

The minimal level of self-determination portrayed in *The Volunteers* is a fictional version of the *Plan X* that Williams analyses in *Towards 2000*. To Williams, if the break-up of the unitary state apparatus is a cause for sadness, this is not because the forms of representative self-determination that have been offered in the nations of Britain have been too dramatically new, but because they have not been far-reaching enough. In 'Are We Becoming More Divided?' Williams writes,

The central point about Scottish and Welsh nationalism is perhaps this: that in Scotland and Wales we are beginning to find ways of expressing two kinds of impulse that are in fact very widely experienced throughout British society. First, we are trying to declare an identity, to discover in fact what we really have in common, in a world which is full of false identities… And second, but related to this, we are trying to discover political processes by which people really can govern themselves – that is, to determine the use of their own energies and resources – as distinct from being governed by an increasingly centralised, increasingly remote and also increasingly penetrating system: the system that those who run it, for their own interests, have decided to call 'Unity'.

Williams does not share in the perceived sadness of the break-up of Britain's united sense of self. Indeed, the promise of devolution movements to bring about co-operative means of control of energy and resources for the people whose lives are determined by them, he sees a real resource of hope. Two points follow from this. Firstly, it can be seen that how political representation is brought about is different in Scotland from Wales. The issues on which the 1979 referenda were fought were very different. Economic policy and especially North Sea Oil being at the heart of the Scottish nationalist movement, while Welsh nationalists campaigned on cultural problems and the Welsh language partly fuelled by a nascent and unaccustomed self-confidence expressed in the 1990s phenomenon of *Cool Cymru*.

Secondly, and even more importantly, Williams suggests that there is an element of similarity-within-difference between the Scottish and Welsh experiences which transcends both of them and is in fact of much wider relevance in British society. To Williams, devolution as a political concept is simply another word for democracy and accordingly allows equal access to the systems of decision and the system of maintenance to people at every level in society. Necessarily, this takes place differently according to the matter being decided and the extent of its reach, so that devolution as a way of ensuring political power at local level offers an ongoing model of similarity within difference. Again in 'Are We Becoming More Divided',

> Once you are not controlled, in advance and systematically, by others, you soon discover the kinds of co-operation, between nations, between regions, between communities, on which any full life depends. But it is then your willing and not your enforced co-operation. That is why I, with many others, now want and work to divide, as a way of declaring our own interests certainly, but also as a way of finding new and willing forms of co-operation: the only kind of co-operation that any free people can call unity.

Co-operation between different political activists at very distinct levels of the community, the wider region and the nation at large hints at Rudolf Bahro's idea of the League of Communists. To Bahro, the objective behind advocating such a League was that it would not only provide connections between different kinds of geographical unit, but that it would also allow for overlap between different political factions. Williams in 'Are We Becoming More Divided?' concludes with a sense of the importance of relating devolution in Scotland and Wales to the long revolution for democracy more generally. But he is not quite able to make any specific proposals for how this could come about. For that, it is necessary to turn again to 'Democracy and Parliament' – and discover the extent to which Bahro's work was developed by Williams' when he wrote it.

Williams, like Bahro, begins 'Democracy and Parliament' by offering to sketch out a series of alternatives to the political system in which he found himself. Like Bahro, this is no simple alternative between capitalism and socialism, however one views either system at the time. Indeed, and with an allusion to the work of Bahro, Williams categorically rejects the two-worlds model of political systems based on economic dichotomy. The real alternatives that Williams develops are based on thinking beyond the inherited electoral system and imagining new forms of political representation, just as Bahro's alternatives involved thinking beyond the bureaucratic milieu in which he worked as trying to propose a wholly new political structure.

To Williams, the whole challenge is typified by his sense of the complex and sometimes contradictory senses of *representation*.

> From very early in their history, there are two related but distinguishable lines of meaning: on the one hand the

process of 'making present'; on the other hand the process of 'symbolization'.

By the former of these, Williams refers to the physical bringing into the places where political decisions are taken people, documents, ideas and evidence pertaining to a particular debate from a physical location that would otherwise be geographically remote from it and hence susceptible to being overlooked. The latter, 'symbolization' is perhaps better characterised as 'typicality' – the process of providing a scaled-down collection of people to form a governing body, in which the human make-up is in direct proportion to the human population of the nation at large 'by locality, by gender, by occupation, by age-group' on a reduced or microcosmic scale. The different sub-cultural groups to which Williams refers indicates that if representation were to be truly democratic, then the governing body of the country would have to represent the people of the country in this typifying way. It is a way that relates closely to Bahro's notion of a League of Communists – an open association of different interest groups.

The notion of interest gives rise in turn to an even more complicated question – the practice of representation, and the vexed question of who or what is being represented, have become if anything more unsatisfactory in the years since 'Democracy and Parliament' was published. In both Scotland and Wales since 1999, electors have had the opportunity to return candidates to their respective Parliament and Assembly using a system of approximate proportional representation known as the 'additional member' system. In this system, electors select a candidate to represent a particular constituency as per the Westminster arrangement – making present the feelings and at times, physical evidence of a particular place at the centre of power. One third of the seats available in each body are then held over for the 'additional member' ballot. Electors cast a second vote, for a particular party rather than a particular individual candidate, and the number of seats won by a party is in proportion to the number of votes it receives. These seats are then allocated to party members according to a pre-arranged list of priority candidates: number one, number two and so on.

The additional member system is a step in the direction of democracy in Scotland and Wales. However, it is not perfect. By garnering support for specific national parties (and the term applies whether we are discussing UK-wide level or the specific nationalist parties of Scotland and Wales) the system militates against a large number of independent candidates being returned to each body. The travesty of this is that it is specifically in the work of independents that the political culture of each nation has developed a particular and effective history. Perhaps in the future, it will become necessary for independent candidates within each nation to find some way of aligning themselves under a banner that is nevertheless not a formally constituted party, in order to participate in the additional member process and have access to the same opportunity of election as the major parties. What would an informal alliance of independent candidates look like if it were not to be a League of some kind, resembling the League of Communists proposed by Bahro – a proposal of which Williams was categorically conscious when he wrote 'Democracy and Parliament'?

At the conclusion of the paper, Williams sets out a series of further proposals which he groups together under three general headings. These are a) interventions in the argument about parliament, b) parliament and other forms of government and c) development in democracy. The first of these is devoted to expanding on the earlier notion of republicanism and the need to bring the real ownership of political power into the hands of the people of the nation. Williams suggests that the monarchy be removed from its role in the political life of the United Kingdom (and implicitly therefore that it be disbanded altogether). This is accompanied by an assertion that the legal category of 'subjects' be replaced by a democratic notion of 'citizens'.

Beyond proposals for altering the system of election to parliament, Williams moves out into a series of proposals for examining the relationship between parliament and other forms of government. It would be simplistic to say that history has overtaken Williams in this area. He notes that 'socialists should propose, and begin acting to ensure, that minority nations and existing regions prepare, by public commission and inquiry, their own proposals for institutions of self-government and representation.' This has indeed, of course, come to fruition to a certain extent since the publication of the paper and since the changes of 1997. Yet the very question of the relationship between parliament at the political centre and the other forms of government that exist in Britain has not been solved by those changes. Indeed, the problems and recurring contradictions have come out into the open and been clarified. 'What is needed, as in the case of "devolution", is that cities and boroughs, counties and districts, should initiate and prepare, including by public inquiry and hearings, their own proposals for democratic reform.' Again, the important point to Williams is that 'old and new problems of local government will not be solved by any handed-down general reform, which would simply confirm the existing relations of power.'

The third series of proposals at the conclusion of 'Democracy and Parliament' return to ideas that inform Williams' long revolution and Bahro's proposed cultural revolution. Industry, education, work, trade unions and other organisations are all implicated. Not only is it through the operation of these organs that Williams hopes to democratise British society. It is also the case that how these organs are run, and for whom, has also to be democratised.

What Raymond Williams built on from his reading of Rudolf Bahro was the importance of avoiding inherited binary models which restrict more critical thinking than they promote. This is evident in his proposals both for reform of the Houses of Parliament, and for relating devolved political power in Scotland and Wales to a more generally extended political franchise. The period since Williams was writing has been characterised by an ongoing and open-ended debate over the role of devolved forms of political power. This is healthy because it demonstrates the activity of a historical process moving away from a simple selection of this system or that.

Williams warns at the conclusion of 'Democracy and Parliament' that a system of devolved government (both in the minority nations and in the regions) 'could go as easily in the direction of a command-bureaucratic government as in the direction of socialist democracy' if its operation becomes contradictory to that of the central government. If this warning of a bureaucratic dictatorship stalling democratic movements recalls Bahro, then the reference becomes explicit in the following sentence: '"actually existing socialism" is of course much nearer the former than the latter.' The Bahro reference in turn tells us not just about the comparability of Williams' thinking on democracy, but actually connotes the kinds of proposal Williams advocates, and which continue to speak to us about the system of political representation in the twenty-first century.

Raymond Williams

Politics and Letters, New Left Books, 1979, Verso, 2015.

'Reflections on Bahro', *New Left Review* 120, 1980.

Towards 2000, Chatto and Windus, 1983.

'Democracy and Parliament', 1982, reprinted in *Resources of Hope*, edited Robin Gable, Verso, 1989.

'Are We Becoming More Divided' (1973–1976) in *Who Speaks for Wales? Raymond Williams*, edited Daniel Williams, UWP, 2003.

Other works

Rudolf Bahro, *The Alternative in Eastern Europe*, New Left Books, 1978.

Hywel Dix, *After Raymond Williams*, 2008, UWP, 2013.

Tom Nairn, *The Break-Up of Britain*, New Left Books, 1977.

9

Resources for a journey of hope

Stephen Woodhams

In a book where the intention has been to locate its subject as of and concerning Wales but then moving beyond, concluding with an essay on research may hopefully encourage others to follow Raymond Williams outwards in directions that make new connections. The comprehensive and indispensable bibliography compiled by Alan O'Connor, which first appeared in 1989, remains a start point. Here it is hoped the scope for commentary afforded by the length of an essay, may better illustrate the many and varied forms through which Williams communicated and so the emphasis is deliberately with material other than conventional published writing. Strangely, given Williams' long involvement with visual and audio work, there is to date no complete listing of Williams: the scriptwriter, playwright, production advisor, presenter and speaker. It is not intended here to provide a comprehensive listing of audio and visual work, and given that broadcast materials are more ephemeral than published work, it may not be possible now to compile a full list. Any such attempt would have to begin with the Raymond Williams Papers now archived and catalogued in Swansea, which includes notices of broadcasts, albeit sometimes as no more than a newspaper cutting, though these may have to serve in the absence of more formal record. The latter part of the chapter cites online references where work associated with the name Raymond Williams can be reviewed at greater length. It may be through online sources that readers will be best able to gauge the extensiveness of Williams' influence across so many concerns, and importantly, his very contemporary relevance. It is also worth considering that at the moment Williams died, the internet was being realised, albeit by only a very few, as a means that could transform communications, and even disrupt senses of knowledge, time and permanency. It is not unreasonable to speculate that Williams' critical reception to the still-emerging technologies, offered for example through fibre optics, would have carried with it a sense of a utopian promise for social relations. It can only be regretted that *The Fight for Manod* where Williams might have further illustrated this part of his thinking, was substantially reduced in length. Ironically, we have descriptions of people in the novel but not the main character, Manod, the city of a new kind.

Ranging across literary criticism, social history, fiction, scripts for drama and film, a regular television column, interviews, contemporary politics, innumerable reviews and a distinctive style of writing theoretically that came across as active thinking, the diversity of Raymond Williams is as remarkable as the volume. The conventional bibliography placed here at the start is, in the main, restricted to selected books. Throughout much of his life Chatto and Windus was Raymond Williams' publisher, and the chronological order is by year of original publication with many of the dates given referring to their list. Details of the latest edition of a work are also given, many of which are in print, and an increasing number including *Second Generation* and *Loyalties*, may also be found as e-books. Of innumerable shorter pieces of writing, those cited at the end of previous chapters may be found among the edited collections discussed after the short bibliography.

Reading and Criticism, Frederick Muller, 1950, reprinted 1962.

Drama Ibsen to Eliot, 1952, Penguin, 1964.

Drama in Performance, 1954, Open University, 1991.

Preface to Film, with Michael Orrom, Film Drama, 1954.

'Culture is Ordinary', 1958, reprinted in *The Raymond Williams Reader*, Blackwell, 2001.

Culture and Society, 1958, Spokesman, 2013.

Border Country, 1960, Library of Wales, Parthian, 2006.

The Long Revolution, 1961, Parthian, 2011.

Second Generation, 1964, Hogarth, 1988.

Modern Tragedy, 1966, 1979. Broadview Press, 2006.

Drama from Ibsen to Brecht, 1968, Hogarth, 1987.

The Country and the City, 1973, Spokesman, 2011.

Television, Technology and Cultural Form, 1974, Routledge, 2003.

Keywords, 1976, 1983, Fourth Estate, 2014.

The Volunteers, 1978, Library of Wales, Parthian, 2011.

The Fight for Manod, 1979, Hogarth, 1988.
Politics and Letters, 1979, Verso, 2015.
Problems in Materialism and Culture, 1980, republished as *Culture and Materialism*, Verso, 2010.
Towards 2000, Chatto and Windus, 1983.
Writing in Society, 1983, Verso, 1991.
Loyalties, 1985, Hogarth Press, 1989.
The Politics of Modernism, 1989, Verso, 2007.
People of the Black Mountains, 1: The Beginning, 1989, Paladin, 1990.
People of the Black Mountains, 2: The Eggs of the Eagle, 1990, Paladin, 1992.
A number of the above titles can be obtained through the Welsh Book Council site, gwales, http://www.gwales.com/home/

Publishers with new editions often as e-books, of Williams' titles or books about Williams, on their lists include:
Parthian Books, http://www.parthianbooks.com/
Spokesman Books, http://www.spokesmanbooks.com/
University of Wales Press, http://www.uwp.co.uk
Lawrence and Wishart, https://www.lwbooks.co.uk/
Verso Books, http://www.versobooks.com/
Broadview Press, https://broadviewpress.com/
Routledge, http://www.routlege.com/
Penguin Books Australia, https://www.penguin.com.au/

Instrumental in bringing to a wider readership the relationship between Wales and Raymond Williams have been two books. *Who Speaks for Wales? Raymond Williams*, edited by Daniel Williams, is the starting place, containing as it does the most complete collection of the writer's commentary on his country. *Raymond Williams: A Warrior's Tale*, by Dai Smith, is the authorised biography of the writer; using the papers he collected and subsequently deposited in Swansea on behalf of the Williams family. Just as the present book is much indebted to Daniel Williams and Dai Smith for their labours so too will be future research.

Edited collections of Raymond Williams' writings include:
Resources of Hope, edited Robin Gable, Verso, 1989.
What I Came to Say, Hutchinson, 1989.
Border Country: Raymond Williams in Adult Education, edited John McIlroy & Sallie Westwood, National Institute for Adult and Continuing Education, 1993.
The Raymond Williams Reader, edited John Higgins, Blackwell, 2001.
Tenses of Imagination, edited Andrew Milner, Peter Lang, 2011.
Raymond Williams on Culture and Society: Essential Writings, edited Jim McGuigan, Sage, 2014.
Raymond Williams: A Short Counter Revolution: Towards 2000 Revisited, edited Jim McGuigan, Sage, 2015
Politics and Culture: Class, Writing, Socialism, edited Phil O'Brien, Verso, 2021

There are refreshing variances between the volumes, so that together their content offers a range of Williams' concerns.

Yet there remain absences, notably drama. *Resources of Hope* presents Williams as a political writer, while including theoretical investigations in areas of culture and the social order. In contrast, *What I Came to Say* and *Tenses of Imagination*, emphasise literary output. The latter is focused on a utopian strain in some writings, while the former has a title that perhaps best describes how Raymond Williams offered himself and his work. The structure of *The Raymond Williams Reader* combines chronology with stages of development to suggest a model for Williams' writing, one that assumes a passage from criticism and culturalism, to abstraction, structure and theory, organised as early to mature works. The two volumes edited by Jim McGuigan are very different in character. The words '*Culture and Society*' in the title of the first, might suggest content reminiscent of Williams' early and famous work of the same title. In fact, the new collection goes further, to include writings denoting not only Williams as a lead figure in the theory of media and communications but also for his advance of sociological theory. The second volume is unusual. It is Williams' *Towards 2000*, edited though to replace a chapter taken from his earlier *The Long Revolution*, with an essay by McGuigan demonstrating the contemporary relevance of the book. Illustrating Williams' uncanny ability to detect future developments, the cogent example, is contemporary neo-liberalism, which, in *Toward 2000*, is memorably captured in Williams' 'Plan X'. *Politics and Culture*, edited by Phil O'Brien, and to be published in the centenary year of Williams' birth, promises to be a potentially remarkable collection. Contained are writings never before published, including for the first time, the full text of 'When Was Modernism', a lecture given in Bristol in 1987.

Finally, a collection requiring longer description; not least because of the inclusion of a significant document. Containing writings that encapsulate in-embryo themes that were to remain central for the rest of his life and to which he contributed more than anyone, *Border Country: Raymond Williams in Adult Education* is unique and invaluable. Essays, letters, notes on classes, discussion of curriculum and subject matter and submissions on teaching methods are all included, making it the most comprehensive testimony of Raymond Williams the teacher. The remarkable document is the Report of a course Williams convened in Oxford for tutors and academics. 'Literature in Relation to History 1850–1875' was held in 1950, yet his write up of the event contains a manifesto for a social history that would aspire to addressing culture as a complex whole. In reality, such a history was not realised for perhaps a further twenty years; in the present work the development is traced with the emergence of Llafur. In my own *History in the Making*, Williams' relations with historians in the 1950s received passable attention, yet there remains need for a detailed examination of his association with the advance made in historical research in Wales and beyond through the whole of that decade. The figure captured by John McIlroy and Sallie Westwood in this edited collection is one setting out on the path that led to the writer he became. Together, *Border Country: Raymond Williams in Adult Education*, *Who*

Speaks for Wales? and *A Warrior's Tale*, afford comprehensive grasp of first the making of Raymond Williams, then years later of the figure that reaffirmed that making; moving back to the border and taking up problems presented for the Welsh internally and in Europe more widely.

The greater part of his unpublished writing together with notebooks, diaries and letters, now constitute the Raymond Williams Papers held within the Archives of Swansea University Library. Ranging across all facets of his life and work, the papers represent the core resource for research. Information about the collection and access is obtainable from Katrina Legg, Raymond Williams Collection, Richard Burton Archives, email: archives@swansea.ac.uk. Though an absence of links between parts of the university website has previously frustrated access, a summary of the content of the Raymond Williams Papers may be found at http://archives. swan.ac.uk/Overview.aspx while a fuller description is at http://archives.swan.ac.uk/Record.aspx?src=CalmView.Catalog&id=WWE%2f2&pos=3. The catalogue meanwhile is at http://archives.swan.ac.uk/TreeBrowse.aspx?src=CalmView. Catalog&field=RefNo&key=WWE%2f2, from where it is possible to access a listing of the entire collection. Cataloguing of the collection was made possible by the Barry Amiel and Norman Melburn Trust, http://www.amielandmelburn. org.uk. The Trust has made possible various educational projects including digitisation of publications relevant to Raymond Williams that are otherwise difficult to access. An introduction to the papers is available as *The Raymond Williams Collection*, edited by Stephen Woodhams. At the time of writing, the future of the coronavirus pandemic is unknowable, and there can be no certainty as to when access to the physical archive at Swansea will be possible. The situation, of course, is global and will inevitably lead archives to digitising their collections. The very real danger is that online availability will see digitised collections gaining attention among researchers while others are marginalised. It is thus incumbent on those interested in seeing Raymond Williams remaining present in the twenty-first century to ensure that a programme of digitising the Raymond Williams Papers is completed at the earliest opportunity.

An extended description of the papers and the forming of the collection can be found at https://www.swansea.ac.uk/crew/research-projects/the-raymond-williams-papers/. CREW, the Centre for Research into the English Literature and Language of Wales, is acknowledged as an international leader in this and related fields of literary and cultural study and oversees a coherent nucleus of relevant enquiry. Dai Smith was appointed to a Research Chair within CREW in 2000 and, with agreement, supervised the complete handover to the University of the Raymond Williams' Papers on completion of his biography, *A Warrior's Tale*, in 2008. CREW consequently facilitate projects associated with the work of Raymond Williams and attract researchers seeking to use the deposited papers. A significant collaboration has been that with institutions in Japan; now amounting to at least five events, the first in 2009, under the heading 'Raymond Williams in Transit' in Tokyo and Swansea. Essential to the venture, Raymond Williams

Kenkyukai (the Society for Raymond Williams Studies in Japan) serves as a means of organising activities and securing funds from Japan Women's University and a Grant-in-Aid for Scientific Research, http://www.jwu.ac.jp/content/files/grp/lecture_news/2010/20100925.pdf. The pulling together of people at Kwansei Gakuin University and elsewhere has helped cohere a forum for seminars and presentations, where Williams can be examined through questions offered by the history and society of Japan. This collaborative venture is perhaps one that could extend to engage participants from other parts of the world, so laying a foundation for further exchanges. Further research at Swansea meanwhile has been promoted through a Raymond Williams Discussion Group, http://crewswansea.blogspot.co.uk/2015/10/raymond-williams-discussion-group.html, that has already attracted contributions from significant figures in the field. Together with the presence of the collected papers, this latest seminar series, on top of the collaboration with Japan, substantiates the ongoing place of CREW in the study of Raymond Williams. The publishers Parthian now share the same site. Parthian in turn had from 2006 the support of the Welsh Government in Cardiff to publish the Library of Wales series, details of which appear below, with 50 volumes published with Dai Smith as series editor to 2016. In addition to promoting the kinds of further work discussed so far, this joining of the Papers, CREW and Parthian in one institutional place, may if suitably supported by other bodies, make it possible to address the pressing questions of how copyright can be secured to ensure more of Williams' texts are kept in print and how writing presently difficult to access can be made available to the general public whether in hard copy or e-format.

A much smaller collection of Raymond Williams' papers, again including some unpublished writings is held at the National Library of Wales, Aberystwyth. Dating from an earlier family deposit the National Library papers now augment those in Swansea and it may be that some cross-referencing between the archives has become necessary. Details of the holding may be found at https://archives. library.wales/downloads/raymond-williams-papers.pdf and access to the papers is available from https://archives.library. wales/index.php/raymond-williams-papers

Interviews with Raymond Williams have appeared in various places, the most extensive forming *Politics and Letters*. Essential to researchers, the book has understandably been quoted many times since its appearance in 1979. Combining biography with political, theoretical and critical answers, the text provides a close insight into the writer and his work. Despite the distortion resulting from an exaggerated tendency to load questions with political reference, *Politics and Letters,* republished in 2015, continues to be the necessary companion to Dai Smith's biography *A Warrior's Tale*, the Daniel Williams edited collection, *Who Speaks for Wales?* and the McIlroy and Westwood edited collection, *Border Country*. It is interesting to compare that book-length interview with more regular examples. 'Decentralism and the politics of place' has been republished in *Who Speaks for Wales?* The original, however, had been an interview with

Philip Cooke completed in January 1984 and published that year in *Radical Wales*. Where nation or nationalism do not even make entries in the index of *Politics and Letters*, in the short shift of time and place to the interview for *Radical Wales* the issues are brought centre stage. We may then contrast again two interviews that would be among the last Raymond Williams gave. 'The Practice of Possibility' was completed with Terry Eagleton at Saffron Walden in 1987 and published in the *New Statesman* for 7 August that year. The interview was republished as 'The Politics of Hope' in *Raymond Williams: Critical Perspectives*. Cause for the interview was the General Election of that year, though subjects ranged wider. Also from that year was an interview for *Planet: The Welsh Internationalist*. Raymond Williams had been living in Craswall adjacent to the Black Mountains and a short distance north from Pandy for twenty years, and the interview concerned the last and unfinished work, *People of the Black Mountains*. Williams speaks of researching the book, and how material evidence of early people requires an understanding of what is being looked at for it to be recognised. Echoes can be found in the novel, where the grandfather, Elis, is presented as someone with intimate knowledge of the mountains and collector of pieces that witness to their past inhabitants. When then his grandson, Glyn, sets out to find the older man, we get description of how what at first sight were stones and rock could be recognised and become bearers of earlier times. Thus with its tighter focus on the form of the novel and its research the interview contrasts in manner with those of *Politics and Letters* a decade earlier. There is too a sense that the interviewer John Barnie, and Raymond, effect an understanding based on their common origins in the border country and the mountains, which helps an easier entry into the geography described and the history unearthed. So it is that, though appearing in the same year, the interviews with *Planet* and for the *New Statesman* offer us contrasting features of Raymond Williams. The directly political interview in Saffron Walden showed his fundamentals had not been changed for short-term expediency. Yet it is the interview with John Barnie in Craswall that offers perhaps best insight to the writer's later years, the integrity of a commitment to his own border country and completion of a work that set out from the historian's facts, then went on to give them meaning.

Raymond Williams' visual and audio work includes screenwriter, appearance in film documentaries and interviews, and contributions in direction and expert advice. Strangely, visual and audio recordings are absent from the superb Bibliography compiled by Alan O'Connor for his *Writing, Culture, Politics*. There is then the oddity that in his *Raymond Williams: On Television*, no references to actual broadcasts appear. An unsatisfactorily partial list of Williams' audio and visual work can be found in *Raymond Williams: Film, TV, Culture*, offered jointly by the National Film Theatre and British Film Institute. There is, however, a further listing available through the British Film Institute database covering not only audio and visual work but also articles and press cuttings relating to Williams, http://collections-search.bfi.org.uk/web. The inclusion of interviews and other contributions by Williams makes the database a significant part of existing records, albeit one that is time-consuming to search. There is then something of an irony that a figure who contributed so much to our understanding of media in varied forms should not have his own creative work as adequately recorded as has been done for the scripts and related materials among the papers in Swansea. Here, only a selected list can be provided, relevant to the themes of the book but still offering a sense of this under-realised dimension of Williams' life.

Public Enquiry, BBC1 tx 15/3/67 and *A Letter from the Country*, BBC1 tx 4/4/66 were each a 'Wednesday Play' written by Williams. *So That You Can Live*, Cinema Action, 1982, drew on Williams as advisor and in quotation. An interview and discussion with Raymond Williams about *So That You Can Live* and his wider concerns with film, appears in *Screen*, 23, 3–4, 1982. Williams' appearances on film include three works directed by Mike Dibb, http://www.mikedibb.co.uk/. The major production is *The Country and The City*. If the recently republished book shares the same title, the film is distinct. Visual image and spoken word allow for extension beyond the written, as with the use of Tatton Park in the English midlands. The area had been the site of the Tatton Estate, and by juxtaposition of image and speech the past of the estate is brought to view so that we see its wealth drawn through tentacles that extended from Manchester in England to expropriations from the plantations of the Caribbean. Joy Williams worked as one of the researchers for the film, while Raymond appears, as in the footage shot by the railway at Pandy, and as a voice reading extracts from pastoral verse. The producer Mike Dibb continues to support *The Country and The City* with presentations and the film is available online. The shorter films were part shot in Cambridge and involved Williams speaking on John Ruskin and William Morris. In each Williams appears, speaking to camera, in what might be his college rooms. The films differ, in that on Ruskin the greater part of the footage focuses elsewhere, in particular on craft workers chiselling stone in what may be some part of the University. In it we hear the voice of a young worker, and the message is clear, his craft and its creative expression afford another way of life that can sit alongside the scholar's whose craft is the transcribing of text first one way, before being offered back another. By contrast, in the William Morris film, it is the interview with Williams that is central. In line with the general title, *Memories of the Future*, the theme is one that remains problematic. The meaning of work, significant in William Morris, reoccurs with Williams, and in the interview he extends the earlier figure's argument, pointing out that work directed only to greater production fails to address a human need for realising creative expression and gaining a sense of self-worth. *Memories of the Future* are, together, two short films that exhibit the profitable working relationship between Mike Dibb and Raymond Williams, and how the latter's contribution to audio and visual production was vital to his means of communication.

A very original work, *A Journey of Hope* broadcast on C4, combined drama based on scenes from his work, excerpts from his novels and interviews with those who knew him. The bringing together of these forms creates a work that can offer an audience without detailed knowledge an insight into a number of consistent themes. Those interviewed are drawn from various parts of Williams' life, so filling out the subject's life. Performed by actors, the readings from novels take on enhanced power, their language given a resonance and emphasis that complements their depth of meaning. However, given our familiarity with the art form, it is perhaps in the drama that issues, persuasively presented, may best engage the widest audience. *Divided Kingdom*, completed as documentaries and subsequently as essays encompasses Wales, though it is not in that episode that Williams appears, but in conversation with Kim Howells for the programme 'home counties'. We meet Williams again at Cambridge where he speaks of the University's connection to other centres of power in London, toward which in the manner of honking geese, to paraphrase his description, some fly.

Landscapes of culture was staged at Birkbeck College in 2018. Among the screenings of Raymond Williams films was a work now little available. *One Pair of Eyes: Border Country* dates from 1967–1970. One scene is that of Williams walking and talking with Dennis Potter with whom he shared a deep affiliation that went back many years. Raymond Williams is heard reflecting on his own life, growing up in border country, his father's work on the railway and the many types of borders that he has and continued to cross in everyday experience. They are themes that have been returned to across the chapters in this book, and the fact that they are so pertinent to experiences for many today reinforces the need to have Raymond Williams' insights and thinking made available for online viewing.

Filmed interviews include an 'in conversation with' Michael Ignatief, about the then recently published novel *Loyalties*. Recorded in possibly 1985 at the Institute of Contemporary Arts, Williams discusses the characters, their parts in the narratives and the linking themes. It is a difficult novel, with its chronological yet widely separated acts, and, inside these, the scenes, each set in one of a number of places, and then in turn the characters who live there or pass through them. Hearing Williams expound on a novel in this manner is not common and perhaps accounts, at least a little, why he is for many almost exclusively a writer of non-fiction. One of the few surviving films of Raymond Williams giving a lecture is that recorded at Letchworth, England in 1984. Titled 'Ecology and the Labour Movement', the talk was presented to an environmental research group with which Williams was actively engaged. The lecture can be seen at https://www. raymondwilliamsfoundation.org.uk/. A BBC Four television series *Great Thinkers: In Their Own Words* moved in its third and final episode to what it rather graphically described as 'The Culture Wars', https://www.bbc.co.uk/programmes/b013fbf0. In the programme description, Raymond Williams is situated alongside Susan Sontag, C.L.R. James and others who denied the reserving of 'culture' to any selective tradition.

Such an alignment better identifies Raymond Williams' place in the tide of the twentieth century.

Few of Raymond Williams' audio recordings have survived; demonstrating that like visual material, audio does not receive the archive and library care of the printed word. Those that remain include holdings by the Open University and that at the National Sound Archive. The BBC it seems randomly lose broadcasts so that audio recordings, such as those for the Third Programme, may just be lost. The loss is greater given that talks on dramatists, and in particular Henrik Ibsen for the Third Programme were among the first contributions by which Raymond Williams became known to a wider public. There is, however, now an annotated record of Williams' broadcasts for the Third Programme the Home Service and later BBC Radio 3 and Radio 4. The records have been made through the BBC Genome Project, which scanned pages from the *Radio Times* to present description of a programme and broadcast. The Project's records suggest that Raymond Williams' first ever broadcast was in December 1949 and titled 'Ibsen's non-theatrical plays'. It is a remarkable biographical citing. Williams had only graduated in 1946, the same year the Third Programme started, and been a Staff Tutor with the Oxford Delegacy for only two years and yet was already being granted time on what was a highly esteemed station with however limited broadcasting hours. Two further talks on Ibsen occurred in 1950, and in February 1951 a talk entitled 'Reading and Criticism'. His book of the same name had been published the previous year, and the programme's description suggests he would have drawn on his own teaching experience. Most of Williams' early broadcasts were for the Third Programme though there are two broadcasts with the Home Service – one citing *Culture and Society* – from 1960 and 1961. The recapturing of these broadcasts through letters, by Dai Smith in *A Warrior's Tale*, offers a valuable connection to this part of Williams' early post-war life.

Programmes in which Raymond Williams, his *Keywords*, legacy and influence are discussed may be found via the BBC website. The advent of BBC Sounds is making more of these programmes available and a limited online archive at least may yet be realised. *Nightwaves* with Philip Dodd was of particular value and in discussing Raymond Williams, Dodd's guests included Terry Eagleton and Stefan Collini. Elsewhere in other programmes engaging with Williams, presenters include Melvyn Bragg, Laurie Taylor and Michael Rosen. One programme of particular relevance to this book, and now available on BBC Sounds was from the World Service. 'Development Dreams: Culture' is described as follows:

There are more than 100 ways to define culture. Dr Rajiv Shah from UNESCO uses the Raymond Williams inter-pretation from his book *Key Words*. Angeline Kamba from the World Commission on Culture and Development also contributes.

UNESCO is exactly where Raymond Williams should be found; the thinker from whom policy and projects may draw.

A related programme, 'Welsh Culture' was first broadcast 27 September 1975 on Radio 3 and is included in *Who Speaks for Wales?* Given only a few years after Williams made re-engagement with Wales obvious, the talk perhaps also signalled the culture of politics inside Plaid Cymru. 'Art: Freedom as Duty', originally a contribution to a symposium at Gregynog Hall, Newtown in September 1978, is available online from *Planet, the Welsh Internationalist* at http://www. planetmagazine.org.uk/audio_visual/raymondwilliams. html. A recording not broadcast but available through the Workers' Education Association, was a talk given at a celebration to mark the work of his Extra-Mural colleague, Tony McLean. 'Adult Education and Social Change' was subsequently published in *What I came to Say*, and is one of the few instances when Williams spoke of his years teaching in south-east England.

Two films offering biographical studies of Williams are *Read All About Us: Raymond Williams*, commissioned by Dai Smith, as Head of Programmes, for BBC Wales and Colin Thomas' *Border Crossing*, BBC Four. Contrasts in the figure presented can serve to remind of the diversity of Williams. The first locates him in terms of Pandy, the Black Mountains and his social roots, giving us a rare visual insight into the environment in which Williams grew up. Colin Thomas' title is apt, and we travel with the young Williams by train from Pandy, through Cambridge toward the international stage that was to become his place among peers. The two films are mirrored here, where our subject is located in a particular history, then in relation to borders across which he communicated and shared so that what was received and offered back, had been enriched. *Raymond Williams – A Tribute*, Large Door, Channel 4, was made possible by a quickly convened round-table screened a few weeks after his death, and included the then President of Plaid Cymru, Dafydd Elis Thomas. Discussion ranged through moments of Raymond's life, speakers recalling times with the writer, such as that by the late Stuart Hall. The place was Raymond Williams' rooms at Cambridge, and Hall recalls how the elevated nature of the setting was felt incongruous by others at the meeting, but how Raymond simply found it a good place to do serious thinking. Stuart Hall's own path through 'England' was one he acknowledges to have been guided by Raymond Williams from the outset.

Among the archive papers in Swansea are descriptions of a range of recordings, typed scripts, transmission dates and correspondence as well as articles. Several items refer to the signally innovative post-war Third Programme mentioned above. The extensive archive listings mean that it is necessary to search under numerous headings for items, but in different places can be found both 'Ibsen's Non-Theatrical Plays' from 1949 and 'Reading and Criticism: An experiment in the teaching of literature', from 1951, each cited earlier in connection with the BBC Genome Project. The archive provides additional information regarding broadcasts and we can gain insight into Williams' own preparations, and why he sought such outlet for his work, especially in the early years before, most obviously, *Culture and Society* propelled him to the position of key cultural commentator on what was, by the early 1960s, a rapidly changing society.

The Keywords Project at http://keywords.pitt.edu/williams_keywords.html, 'is a collaborative research initiative investigating "key" words prominently used in social debate in English.' The web-based project is a development between the universities of Pittsburgh and Cambridge. The core contents are essays on selected words, the editors inviting continuous contributions from writers mindful of the real effect of words both personally and socially. A feature of the project of interest here is the collection of online linked videos with Raymond Williams appearing or associated with themes in his work. Elsewhere this dimension of Williams' life, and attention to audio-visual forms, has been significantly lacking and it is therefore of importance for future understanding of Williams that this singularly rich resource offered by the project be exploited more widely. The Keywords Project is an innovation in keeping with Williams' interest in technology and the possibilities of new forms for social interactions. Its learning potential through exchanges of knowledge is already apparent in what is still a young venture.

Writers and writing on Williams and Wales include Dai Smith, 'Relating to Wales' in *Raymond Williams: Critical Perspectives*, edited by Terry Eagleton (1989); his *Aneurin Bevan and the World of South Wales* (1993), and *In the Frame: Memory in Society 1910–2010* (2010), which if an autobiography in one mode, is also a biography of South Wales in another. Sharing something of the quality of Raymond

Williams, Dai Smith engages the reader so that we are invited to participate in an active process of thinking. He is a figure who for some years has been all too rare: a Public Intellectual. Comprising the first part of *Who Speaks for Wales?* is Daniel Williams' essay, 'The Return of the Native', which provides one of the best responses to Williams from within Wales. It is also a corrective to misunderstandings in the United States and elsewhere, a matter that Daniel Williams has taken further in 'To Know the Divisions: The Identity of Raymond Williams' in *Wales Unchained* which appeared in 2015. A reader wishing to understand Raymond Williams amid contemporary debates needs to work through Daniel Williams whose range of writings now include, '"Insularly English": Raymond Williams Nation and Race' and 'Writing against the Grain: Raymond Williams *Border Country* and the Defence of Realism'. Among his earlier contributions were 'Dai, Kim and Raymond Williams', *Planet*, 114, 1995–6, and, with Ned Thomas and Dai Smith, 'The Relevance of Raymond Williams', *Planet*, 195, 2009. In turn, Ned Thomas' article, 'It is Never the Native Who Returns', can be found in *Planet*, 190, 2008. Among earlier pieces, *The New Welsh Review*, commenced at the time of Williams' death, published in its second issue essays on the novels and on Williams as an inhabitant of Wales. Finally, Jeremy Hooker's 'A Dream of a Country', *Planet* 49/50, 1980, provides an early response to the Welsh trilogy. Together these writers comprise the richest written response to Raymond Williams, though coming as it does from within Wales that is perhaps not a surprise. What they share is a quality of common history, common experience, that enables an empathy which those addressing Williams from afar perhaps cannot replicate. It is a quality we shall meet again when turning to visual engagement with the border country and the environment that informed Williams' early life.

Other complete works on Raymond Williams are varied as to theme and temperament. Of interest here are John Powell Ward, *Raymond Williams*, Writers of Wales, 1981; Tony Pinkey, *Raymond Williams*, 1991; Hannu Nieminen, *Communication and Democracy: Habermas, Williams and the British Case*, 1997; Paul Jones, *Raymond Williams's Sociology of Culture*, 2004; Alan O'Connor, *Raymond Williams*, 2006 and Hywel Dix, *After Raymond Williams*, 2013. The writers focus on different elements of Williams, so that readers must move between the volumes if they are to appreciate not only the acknowledged breadth, but also, how Williams' work connects. Ward's book offers a useful introduction though sadly there is a lack of biographical context. As one of the few attempts to address Williams' novels, Tony Pinkey's is a valuable contribution, and indeed audacious in claiming a post-structuralist path onwards from an early realism.

Hannu Nieminen's *Communication and Democracy: Habermas, Williams and the British Case* is an unusual work and its relevance to the present work makes it deserving of longer comment. Firstly because, published in 1997, it was ahead of others in bringing together Habermas and Williams. It is perhaps also unusual in stemming from a Finnish origin though owing much to the then intellectually powerful Centre for Communication and Information Studies at the University of Westminster. That it was here that much of the work for the book was carried out is not surprising. The Centre had been something of a bridge with Victor Burgin pointing toward Susan Sontag in one direction and a host of figures pointing toward Raymond Williams in another – Nicholas Garnham for instance directed the film *One Pair of Eyes: Border Country*. Hannu Nieminen's book discusses communications and democracy, the former primarily in terms of media. The discussion ranges over theoretical considerations and historical exploration of how communications and democracy have developed in relation to each other in Britain. In pursuing Habermas and Williams' response to this question, Hannu Nieminen adopts a somewhat textbook structure for the book with many headings slicing up the account so that the reader may take each piece in limited bite-size chunks. *Communication and Democracy* therefore may also serve to bring Habermas and Williams before readers who may be familiar with only one of Nieminen's subjects.

The gap in years to Paul Jones' book is perhaps significant, for the Raymond Williams that emerges in this later work is a sociologist. Evidently, this is not the narrower academic use of the term, but rather a thinker whose breadth takes in the social whole, and thus sits alongside generations of peers from Wilhelm Dilthey and Max Weber, through Walter Benjamin and Karl Mannheim, Lucien Goldmann and Pierre Bourdieu to Jürgen Habermas. The book suggests the direction pursued here in chapters seven and eight where

Williams is situated among twentieth-century European thinkers. Alan O'Connor's 2006 book is a further addition to his earlier studies, and while primarily concerned with media, offers a plausible case for Williams' later years to share greater sympathy for anarchist thinking than has usually been allowed. Questioning how to approach Williams, O'Connor discusses the singularity of *History in the Making* by Stephen Woodhams which locates Williams not as the lone figure he is often characterised as being, but as part of a generation, a description perhaps closer to Williams' sense and presentation of himself as being of a society. Written a slightly later again, Hywel Dix's book, *After Raymond Williams* (2008), takes its start point from Williams, moving on through a range of continental theories in exploring the implications for the United Kingdom of pressures toward devolution and even federalism. The trajectory over the years traversed by these books is a steady movement out, liberating their subject from the confines of an Anglo-focused world of English literature, to better test Williams' contribution to related thinking in Europe. A necessary next step is the move beyond even that geographical confine.

Collections of essays on Raymond Williams are varied in quality and a helpful assessment can be found in Daniel Williams' Introduction to *Who Speaks for Wales?* Illustrative collections that provide divergent insights into the range of work are *Raymond Williams: Critical Perspectives*, edited by Terry Eagleton (1989); *Raymond Williams, Politics, Education, Letters*, edited by John Morgan and Peter Preston, (1993), and *About Raymond Williams*, edited by Monika Siedl et al.,

(2010). The Critical Perspectives collection was compiled in discussion with Williams who, as Terry Eagleton recalls in a personal introduction, had been due to write an 'Afterword'. It is appropriate that in writing of a figure as much of the future as the past, the contributors' tenses remained unaltered by his death. *Politics, Education, Letters* contains still too rare essays on the years in adult education and an interesting discussion of 'Williams' fictional Wales'. The accessible manner of the essays in this collection make it suitable as an introduction to the man as well as to the writing.

About Raymond Williams brings together contributors from across Europe, so making for a fuller measure of Williams than earlier English-focused responses had achieved. The geographic spread of the collection takes Williams' ideas into new territories, testing them with fresh rigour. An example is that by Clara Masnatta, 'Raymond Williams in the South Atlantic'. In fact, the essay brings out the reception of Williams in South America and in particular Argentina, where a working through of divisions, literary – cultural – political, to a point where, in the course of at times totalitarian oppression, a continuity of themes could be established. The essay is also a protest against a North American colonialism wherein cultural studies as defined in the United States is the rubric through which the 'south' is interpreted. If the present work succeeds in connecting Wales to the essays in *About Raymond Williams*, it may have afforded a productive association.

Following on from *About Raymond Williams*, we can

turn to a book to be published in 2021. *Raymond Williams at 100* is obviously a celebration of the centenary, though the collected essays are by younger writers or those bringing fresh questions to Williams' work. A brief example is the essay by the editor, Paul Stasi, 'Inexplicable goodness: Raymond Williams, Charles Dickens and The Ministry of Utmost Happiness'. The connection with Arundhati Roy mirrors my own in 'Crossing Borders' in *Kenkyu*, 9, 2020. In that essay the connection drawn is that between *Border Country* and *The God of Small Things*. Connecting Arundhati Roy and Raymond Williams may yet prove to be a source of fruitful enquiry. Similarly timed for the centenary, a forthcoming issue of the online journal *Coils of the Serpent* is devoted to Williams. The origin of the issue lay with a conference in Potsdam in January 2018. Both conference and issue of the journal carry the title 'Beyond Crisis' and, like *About Raymond Williams* and *Raymond Williams at 100*, the emphasis is on new or younger writers making fresh uses of Williams' ideas.

Lectures have long been a feature connected with the name Raymond Williams. Their origins are various and reflect widespread belief that Williams' own manner of offering his thoughts spoken out loud to engage response should continue. Appropriately, the lectures have not been uniformly regular in place and time but occur sometimes as standalone events or else as key talks at a more extended gathering. The Raymond Williams Lecture in Wales began in 1989, with Dai Smith as speaker. The title 'Raymond Williams and His Country' points to a continuity of concern with Wales and the border country, one echoed by numerous speakers down the years. The lecture in Wales has been given by speakers who recall the associations Raymond built. Stuart Hall and Terry Eagleton for instance were friends and their contributions might be expected. In 1996 though, it was the turn of Michael D. Higgins from Ireland, the then minister for culture, and the country's future President. His talk, subsequently published *The Migrants Return* was organised by Dai Smith for BBC Wales. At least three Assembly Members (now known as Members of the Senedd) have spoken, while the last speaker in that particular lecture series was Alan Tucket, a Director of the National Institute for Adult Continuing Education in 2005. The range is significant and surely right, reflecting the way that Williams spent considerable time speaking outside the enclosed walls of the academy, reaching out so that, to differing publics, the name Raymond Williams conveys associations that only an understanding of the man can connect. A list of this first series of lectures may be found via the Raymond Williams Foundation website.

In 2015, the Raymond Williams Memorial Lecture in Wales was revived. In its revived form the annual lecture would seem to be a stage where influential figures have the opportunity to expound a case, and where at least one section of the intended audience is other significant figures. Those involved have included Members of Senedd, and a University Vice-Chancellor. The formal manner of the renewed lectures may be a sign that the general renewed interest in Raymond Williams is attracting official as well as popular attention. A parallel lecture is that staged as part of the annual Hay-on-Wye literature festival. Speakers have been diverse with appropriately a greater presence of writers and global reach. Hanif Kureshi spoke in 2003 on silencing voices of dissent. Four years later in 2007 Wole Soyinka spoke on a related theme, 'Writing on the Wall of Silence'. There may in each have been an echo of the 1995 talk by Eric Hobsbawm on twentieth-century extremism, following his celebrated book *The Age of Extremes*. The Hay Lecture is perhaps a means for global responses to Williams to be publicly offered, and the potential to share differing experiences is evident. It is just such an extended geographic and experiential reach that efforts to mark the centenary of Raymond Williams birth would do well to build on.

In England, there is the Raymond Williams Lecture at Cambridge University. Open to the public, the lecture offers the opportunity for academics and others to present arguments that draw inspiration from thoughts offered by Williams and which, as he intended, have been taken further. The 2020 Lecture, 'Where in the World is World Literature' was delivered by Homi Bhabha, and the invitation 'All Welcome' on the faculty notice seems particularly fitting for a lecture named after a figure from whom that sentiment would have been genuine. Continuous lectures have been organised by the Raymond Williams Society and the Raymond Williams Foundation. Both bodies were established through appeals after his death in 1988 and each gained support to begin and continue lines of work that are distinct though co-operative. The society lecture varies in location, and in recent years has been coupled with the Annual General Meeting, www.raymondwilliams.co.uk. A list of previous speakers is available from the society's website. Longer conferences in media, literature and culture have been staged, participants reviewing contemporary issues with insights drawn from Williams' work. In 2015, the society staged an innovative event 'Raymond Williams Now' in Manchester with examples of how Williams speaks to artists working in contemporary creative fields. The society's journal *Key Words* has had a long association with the Russell Press which traces its roots back to the philosopher and peace activist, Bertrand Russell, http://www.spokesmanbooks.com/acatalog/Key_Words_Journal.html.

In 2011, a link between international groups was made when *Key Words* published a collection of essays associated with the seminar series 'Raymond Williams in Transit'. The essays by writers from Japan brought fresh insight and appreciation of Williams' work that perhaps required the impression of a different society from that in which he lived most of his life. What comes through is the universalism of Williams' thinking, a feature perhaps not recognisable within the limiting scope of Britain, or as Dai Smith puts it in his 'Afterword: Found in Translation', 'Sometimes it seems you have to go halfway round the world to gain a fresh perspective on familiar things.'

It is perhaps the shock of recognition that comes through essays from writers across the world. The realisation that, in a very different history and society, those matters of which Williams wrote and spoke have also been directly experienced and are being worked through. What then comes through is that in Japan, the false division between the critical and creative lacks relevance, so that the fresh perspective gained on Williams may be closer to the whole figure. These features in work from Japan perhaps substantiate the endeavour in *From Wales to the World* to, as the title suggests, lose the shackles of 'Cambridge English critic' and embrace the global resonance of its subject as a single whole.

The Raymond Williams Foundation has staged annual Raymond Williams 'weekends' since its inception. The event has often opened with a keynote address that, like the Society lecture, has attracted significant names over the years. The Foundation's website contains details of various activities and a further reading page with articles on new editions of Williams' books and related writings, exhibitions and events http://www.raymondwilliamsfoundation.org.uk. The distinctiveness of the Foundation is a commitment to informal learning with participatory sessions on contemporary issues a feature of its work. It is commitment that has been realised through engagement with populations outside academia, with everyday environments used for small groups. Looking to the future, the Foundation has turned to exploiting advances possible through online virtual groups, and how, by this means informal learning might even be extended to include those with limited access to traditional meetings. The provision of grants and bursaries to individuals and groups has made the Foundation an important supporter of research and includes a 'Reading

Retreat Scheme' that can be taken advantage of at two residential institutes in England. In conjunction with a range
of organisations, primarily based in Wales, the Foundation
has taken a lead role in plans to mark the centenary of
Raymond Williams' birth.

Beyond Dai Smith and Daniel Williams, two further
figures necessary to cite in a book tracing its subject from
Wales are Gwyn Alf Williams and Gwyn Thomas. As a
television historian, Gwyn Alf Williams was perhaps the
single most important figure in presenting a history of Wales
to the outside world. His most engaging work, presented
with the veteran broadcaster Wynford Vaughan Thomas, was
The Dragon Has Two Tongues for Channel 4, which arguably
has yet to be surpassed in this genre of broadcasting. The
fullest biographical treatment of Gwyn Alf Williams is also,
appropriately, through film. Produced by Colin Thomas, *The
Peoples' Remembrancer* is an extended interview interspersed
with episodes from Gwyn Williams' remarkably creative
life, BBC Wales/S4C, 1995. The only biography in print
is *The People's Historian* by Geraint Jenkins, University of
Wales Centre for Advanced Welsh and Celtic Studies,
while a bibliography can be found in the essays presented
to him in *Artisans, Peasants and Proletarians*. Reviews of
Gwyn Alf Williams work by Raymond Williams have
been republished in *Who Speaks for Wales?* That historians
tell us what happened, novelists tell us why, is a truth of
Welsh writing and if Gwyn Alf Williams stands to one
side of Raymond Williams, Gwyn Thomas stands to the
other. More than any other figure Gwyn Thomas captured

a history, fashioned it to his use, then presented it back to the world in a narrative style that was his own. Driven by compassion, his novels and stories capture a pathos of South Wales that can convey both resilience and the absurd in the same moment. A South Wales subjected to social dislocation in the interwar years is the character of much of his writing. There is in these works a technique deployed whereby figures are expressions of their place and time; names are interchangeable, being arbitrary, their collective presence more important than individuality. Novels now available on The Library of Wales list include *The Dark Philosophers*, *The Alone to the Alone* and *All Things Betray Thee*. Raymond Williams contributed the Foreword to a 1986 Lawrence and Wishart edition of *All Things Betray Thee*, which reappears in the volume published under the Library of Wales. In it, Williams comments that the work was perhaps the highest achievement of a form that has come to be referred to as the Welsh Industrial Novel.

At present withdrawn, the Raymond Williams Community Publishing Prize was created in 1989. Funded by Arts Council England, the prize was established to reward published works of 'outstanding creative and imaginative quality that reflected the life and experiences of particular communities'. It was open to not-for-profit publishers and awarded annually. A significant participant in administrating the prize was the Federation of Worker Writers and Community Publishers, a network of groups bringing forward writing that otherwise would not have been accessible to readers. Raymond Williams had contributed to the work of federation members by way of accepting invitations to speak. The prize was particularly notable for rewarding writing politicising sex and gender by consciously working-class women; a type of writing that, being by women foregrounding their working-class consciousness, has been rejected by much of academic feminism. Commencement of a similar prize with renewed funding could serve as a significant incentive for what can be marginalised writing overlooked by established literary awards.

Continuing our emphasis on the creative over the merely critical, *Keywords* is once again the inspiration, only rather than written text the ideas are taken on into the visual arts. The Keywords Lectures at Rivington Place in Shoreditch ran between autumn 2010 and spring 2011. Rivington Place benefits from a library enhanced with a collection donated by Stuart Hall who worked with Raymond through the early years of the New Left and later on for the *May Day Manifesto*. In 2013 at Rivington Place and at Tate Liverpool in 2014, an exhibition was staged offering changes in the use and meanings of Keywords in contemporary society. Presenting Williams' historical semantics in visual forms is a move too little attempted given the writer's involvement in visual media. Keywords has been a collaboration between iniva and Tate, so that further details of lectures and exhibitions are separated between addresses http://www.iniva.org/exhibitions_projects/2013/keywords, http://www.rivingtonplace.org/keywords and http://www.tate.org.uk/whats-on/tate-liverpool/exhibition/keywords-art-culture-and-society-1980s-britain.

Two collections have existed for a number of years, offering researchers opportunity to access Williams' published work and some audio and visual recordings. The collection at Cardiff dates from before the Swansea Archive and holds a possibly unique range of published materials, https://www.cardiff.ac.uk/special-collections/explore/collection/raymond-williams-works. Made possible by Dai Smith, and containing items from Raymond Williams' own library, the collection includes a small number of audio recordings in tape format. The archive at Nottingham was deposited by Merryn Williams, providing possibly the largest resource in England, http://www.ntu.ac.uk/library/resources_collections/special_collections/a-z/index.html.

The Library of Wales, whose appointed series editor was Dai Smith, is a Welsh Government project launched in 2006 to ensure that largely unavailable classic literature in Wales that has been written in English will be made accessible. Books in The Library of Wales appear through Parthian, a publisher now intimately associated with the name of Raymond Williams and, as already noted, located on the campus at Swansea along with the Raymond Williams Papers and CREW. To date two of Williams' novels have been republished by the library, *Border Country* and *The Volunteers*, with forewords by Dai Smith and Kim Howells respectively. Raymond Williams' short story 'The Writing on the Wall' appeared in the collection *Colours of a New Day: Writing for South Africa* in 1990 and was reprinted in *Story II: The Library of Wales Short Story Anthology* in 2013; an earlier story 'A Fine Room to be ill in' from 1948 appeared in the

New Penguin Book of Welsh Short Stories which the South Wales novelist Alun Richards edited in 1993. The Library of Wales has also republished a number of works of what has been called the Welsh Industrial Novel. Gwyn Thomas has already been referred to, but others including Jack Jones and Lewis Jones are significant. The part played by this now recovered tradition in informing Williams' own writing is perhaps not entirely knowable, but *Border Country* was written and structured in response to the perceived limits of this genre of writing in Wales. There are further titles of Williams that should be offered, and it must be hoped the Library of Wales Series, recently halted at some fifty volumes, will be recommenced. The Library of Wales can be found at http://thelibraryofwales.com/.

openDemocracy http://www.opendemocracy.net/about is a successful and popular news and discussion network that offers coverage of contemporary issues and interventions into controversies. It is one of the best examples of the type of work Raymond Williams spoke of as possible with the then embryonic e-technologies coming into existence. Connections with Raymond Williams were demonstrated by Anthony Barnett, creator of openDemocracy,

http://www.opendemocracy.net/anthony-barnett/long-and-quick-of-revolution, and in the foreword to the new edition of *The Long Revolution*, https://www.parthianbooks.com/products/the-long-revolution and in e-format at http://thelibraryofwales.com/node/68. The theme may be followed further through a related journal article 'The Long Revolution Revisited' (Soundings 35, 2007). Its author, Michael Rustin, worked with Raymond Williams through the May Day Manifesto Committee, the Socialist Society and continues to share Williams' programme. His relationship with Stuart Hall – which was also a family relationship – from these earlier interventions was again productive in a now well-known project popularly referred to as the Kilburn Manifesto. William Morris Unbound, edited by Tony Pinkey, carries essays drawing on Raymond Williams' and lines of thinking that connect the two figures, http://williammorrisunbound.blogspot.co.uk/. The site is informally associated with the William Morris Society which Tony Pinkey laments has lost the passion of the Victorian visionary.

The Philippines Matrix Project describes itself as 'Interventions toward a national-democratic socialist transformation'. The idea may be related to Williams' developing commentary on Wales in essays found in *Who Speaks for Wales?* The project website contains essays on a number of figures and their work, and the 'interventions' may be placed in the tradition of 'really useful knowledge'. Among Raymond Williams connected entries are two essays starting with the following address:

http://philcsc.wordpress.com/2008/10/13/raymond-williams-british-public-intellectual. Two further responses to Williams from elsewhere in Asia may be here be contrasted with that from the Philippines Matrix Project. *Raymond Williams through Sri Lankan eyes* is a series by Professor Wimal Dissanayake. Dissanayake had previously been a student of Williams at Cambridge, an experience that

resonates with fondness through the writing. Some four-
teen wide-ranging articles appeared in the *Sunday Observer*
between August 2012 and January 2013, introducing the
figure, discussing themes that typify Williams' work and
demonstrating their relevance to Sri Lanka's contemporary
literary scene. What marks out Wimal Dissanayake's exposi-
tion is the personal empathy and depth of appreciation that
arises from his taking the breadth of Williams writing as a
whole. Each article has a separate web address and readers
would be wise to use the generic title, *Raymond Williams
through Sri Lankan eyes* to locate the series.

Something of the same freshness of perspective might be
said of the 'Chinese Reception of Raymond Williams' (2012);
Yin Qiping's approach is one from which we could learn to
our benefit. The article serves two purposes. The first part
reviews the uptake of Williams in China in the twenty-first
century, and the increased interest is remarkable:,

> The last decade has witnessed a burgeoning literature on
> Raymond Williams in China. In addition to over fifty
> articles, three book-length studies have been published
> since 2001, whereas prior to 2001 there were only two
> essays and one book of this kind.

A particular focus for the increased interest has, a little
too predictably perhaps, been 'cultural materialism', a term
all too often used as a shorthand defining of Williams as
though that were all that needed to be said. However, it
is the second part of Yin Qiping's essay that provides the

'fresh perspective'. Here there is a pushing back against the shorthand, and an all too rare careful exploration of what Williams actually said. In brief, Yin Qiping demonstrates that literary and aesthetic values are essential to Williams. Far from the all-too-ready reductionism to politics etc., that in some hands cultural materialism affords, Williams strenuously argued for the need to respect literary forms and conventions in themselves and even appreciate the lyrical, rhythmic patterns of words that can afford aesthetic value. Yin Qiping has perhaps given us a reminder of Williams' close reading of creative expression and the subtlety of his prose.

Projects and events in the border country, near the Black Mountains have drawn on themes from Williams' novels, perhaps most obviously as they appeared in his last and unfinished work *People of the Black Mountains*. The reach of the writing, covering some twenty thousand years over three volumes, of which tragically only two appeared, has perhaps daunted an adequate response in standard essay form; certainly, the writing defies compartmentalised academia. Rather, and perhaps appropriately, responses have been in visual and spoken form, where the physical presence of the mountains can be better presented. The Diffusion exhibition is based on a collection of photographs taken over several decades through North Wales and the borders that constitute 'a dense visual encounter with place and history.' Drawing on Williams' structure of feeling, Diffusion 'reinforces the power of photography to convey a similar idea of lived experience… at a particular time and

place.' http://2013.diffusionfestival.org/programme-item/
structures-of-feeling-2/. Turning from the visual to the
spoken word, a day school on *People of the Black Mountains*
was held at the Priory Centre, Abergavenny in October 2011.
The event organised for the Raymond Williams Society
brought together figures associated with Williams and the
area, including Elizabeth Allen. The event offered responses
to Williams and exploration of how the Black Mountains
infused a writer who had spoken of how when he closed
his eyes it was their image he saw.

> Press your fingers close on this lichened sandstone. With
> this stone and this grass, with this red earth, this place
> was received and made and remade. Its generations are
> distinct, but all suddenly present.

The words, from *People of the Black Mountains*, inspired
a venture set in the border country that was home to
both a young Jim and a mature Raymond. Diana Heeks'
Black Mountains Project connects with communities
living across the region and is supported by the Creative
Network. The project concluded in an open studio day
with reflection on how the work proceeded. Details of
the project may be found at https://peak.cymru/archive/
diana-heeks-black-mountains-project/.

The border country over which the Black Mountains cast
so imposing a presence has also inspired a more recent visual
response, going back to Williams' first novel. *Ffiniau: Four
painters in Raymond Williams' Border Country* arranges the

work of artists contemporary with Williams and in whose work can be seen themes conveyed otherwise in the novel. First presented at the National Eisteddfod in Abergavenny, the exhibition, curated by Peter Wakelin went on to tour other centres across the country. Writing in *New Welsh Review*, Claire Pickard addressed the concluding event,

> The scheduling of 'Crossing Borders', – the Museum of Modern Art's one-day conference on art and litera-ture, accompanying its new exhibition, 'Four painters in Raymond Williams' *Border Country*' – could hardly have been more timely. The nature of Williams' work made it inevitable that themes of identity and community, and of the relationship between Welshness and Britishness, would dominate such an event. Yet, in the aftermath of the Brexit vote any discussion of such ideas feels particularly charged and pertinent. As the day unfolded, and speaker after speaker reverted to such topics, an unofficial theme for the conference began to emerge – that of the continued and unmistakable relevance of *Border Country*.

It requires no great imagination to appreciate the pertinence of Pickard's references to contemporary events for this book, albeit that their presence has been latent. To have made these events manifest would have meant writing a different work. We might, however, turn to her last line, 'the continued and unmistakable relevance of *Border Country*.' That has been clear here, where contradictions and conflicts over belonging and how that condition is made and remade across time and place can be recognised in several chapters. Then, too, have been questions of borders, their varied forms which we, like Williams, must seek to negotiate in our own lives. Turning back to the exhibition, the originality of using artists contemporary with Williams, rather than current painters responding back through time, is to be welcomed. There was for them perhaps a way of seeing unavailable to a later generation; the intervening years having altered both landscape and, in some regards, how the land is used. Crossing town and country their work echoes concerns that stayed with Williams in the years after that first remarkable novel.

The penultimate entry brings us to a contemporary and even ongoing project. At points in this chapter, comment has been made that audio and visual recordings of Williams have not received the archival attention of his written work and indeed his notes, summaries and even correspondence. That situation has very recently improved substantially thanks to a project where a number of tapes have been digitised and made available for the first time. Briefly, the tapes were in the possession of the Williams family who made them available to the Secretary of the Raymond Williams Society (RWS). A grant from the Amiel and Melburn Trust supported the digitising of audio tapes, and these are available as podcasts for public listening by way of the RWS website https://raymondwilliams.co.uk/. A full description of how the project was completed can also be found on the website. A summary of the materials available reads thus:,

The cassette tapes take five forms: 1) lectures never before transcribed or published; 2) the original recordings of what became essays published in collections such as *Culture and Materialism* (1980) and *Resources of Hope* (1989); 3) the reading of published articles; 4) the dictation by Williams of his fictional work; 5) the full version of texts only ever published in abridged form.

A second archive also held by the Williams family consists of VHS recordings of Williams. As with the audio tapes these too range in content and include both broadcasts and recordings of Williams speaking. An example is a recording of a talk on D. H. Lawrence for the Alternative Video Group in 1985, the nature of which meant that it had only limited accessibility.

This project is without doubt one of the most important advances in making Williams available online, which is essential to our appreciating how this original thinker developed and delivered his ideas in spoken form. The project is led by Phil O'Brien and related to his edited collection of Williams' writings, *Culture and Politics*, (Verso 2021). There is, as O'Brien comments, scope for further work making Williams more accessible in audio and visual formats and is exactly the type of project toward which it is intended this chapter should contribute.

We might, in closing, turn to a field where Raymond Williams has been until relatively recently little acknowledged: urban–agrarian geographies. Essays now appearing contribute to a relocating of Williams among other

European thinkers, the particular case here being that of Henri LeFebvre. A French-born thinker, writer and activist, Henri LeFebvre has probably not received the attention in the Anglo–American world given to others of his countrymen and women. The reasons are as much to do with publishing fashions as any other since these often dictate what appears to be seen by the majority of readers. We may note briefly here a similarity with Raymond Williams whereby each writer was significantly marked by the war when 'Lefebvre was helping the resistance movement to "derail enemy trains" and hunt down Nazi "collaborators".' Experiences that were likely to have been as impressionable as Williams' when the latter was at the spearhead of the dash from the Normandy landings to the crossing of the Rhine by the British Army 1944–45.

'Totality, Hegemony, Difference: Henri LeFebvre and Raymond Williams' by Andrew Shmuely appeared in a collection of papers edited by, among others, Kanishka Goonewardena. Andrew Shmuely chose his title well: the words – totality, hegemony and difference – are pursued carefully in the composition that follows. LeFebvre and Williams are each claimed for an approach that holds to the need for an understanding that can encompass totality yet allow sufficient latitude for difference. It is a feature in his work that will be recognisable even if it also meant a degree of complexity that could leave some readers wishing Williams would be more decisive.

Kanishka Goonewardena's 'The Country and The City in the Urban Revolution' is the first full engagement by the writer with Raymond Williams. Goonewardena acknowledges that to date Williams has not made the impact on urban studies that he should have done. Now, however, with the demise of post-modern initiatives there is need for recapturing a sense of totality that will bring together two hitherto separate worlds, that concerned with the urban and that with the agrarian. It is exactly such a bringing together of the country and the city that Williams sought. The theme has occurred previously in this present book, and it is encouraging that elsewhere the need to unite two disparate worlds and their examination is perhaps beginning to be more appreciated. What we may add here is that where, understandably, Goonewardena concentrates on *The Country and The City*, we might add that the unity of country and city and struggle over land use are perhaps offered to a wider readership in *The Fight for Manod* and *People of the Black Mountains*. The latter part of Kanishka Goonewardena's chapter turns to present day India and the human and environmental destruction being wrought by neo-liberalism in that country. The estimated death by suicide of a farmer every thirty minutes is not the reality of India that Western media enthralled to the 'modernising' drive by the Bharatiya Janata Party (BJP) would like us to be aware of. Neo-liberalism in India is for many fast turning poverty back to an absolute state. The connections drawn with India in Kanishka Goonewardena's chapter enable mention here of a parallel essay accompanying this book that appeared in the Tokyo-published *Raymond Williams Kenkyu*, 9, March 2020. There Raymond Williams is linked with Arundhati Roy, first in terms of overlapping political standpoints and then through *Border Country* and Roy's global phenomenon, *The God of Small Things*. The essay it is to be hoped will point us toward further research on the potential connections between two figures combining writing with a public intellectual presence.

This chapter has been written in the hope too that readers are able to use its resources in ways beneficial to wider and deeper research and therefore take from its random form as specifically appropriate. Far from all available sources have been cited and selection was made in line with emphases in this book. In researching the chapter, it has become clear that an e-catalogue of all audio and visual sources with or on Raymond Williams is urgently needed, as too that of at least substantial online resources with sufficient notes to make the listing informative for its use. In a book setting out from Wales to explore the parameters of Raymond Williams, a Welsh European, it is hoped that this particular chapter has contributed to the establishing of such resources, and so, the international perspective his work requires and demands.

Contributor Biographies

Chapters were written as follows: Stephen Woodhams, one, two, four and nine; Elizabeth Allen, three and five; Derek Tatton, six; and Hywel Dix, seven and eight.

Elizabeth Allen hails from the border country, and her subsequent life in Hastings in the south east of England gives her insight into the tensions and contradictions that Williams at an earlier time had to negotiate. Her engagement with Raymond Williams has taken several forms over a number of years. Her thesis 'The Dislocated Mind: The Fiction of Raymond Williams' emphasises the importance of a realist form and range of genres crossed by his novels. Elizabeth served for several years on the Committee of the Raymond Williams Society and more briefly, the Editorial Board of its Journal, *Keywords*. Elizabeth was for some years a Senior Lecturer in Cultural Studies at Regent's College, London.

Derek Tatton's life and work has followed in the steps of Raymond Williams. Like Williams, Derek came from a working-class background being employed at Crewe Railway Station for several years. Derek attended Coleg Harlech before gaining an Extra-Mural Bursary to Cambridge where he was taught by Williams who also later supervised his Open University PhD. His thesis, 'The tension between political commitment and academic neutrality in the W.E.A.' reflected Williams' own earlier concerns with the purposes of adult education. For many years Derek was Warden/Principal of Wedgwood Memorial College. After Williams' death, Derek was the lead figure in establishing the Raymond Williams Foundation and its commitment toward open and democratic learning. Over time Derek has nurtured the Foundation to the point where now it supports annual weekends, provides grants for educational projects in the UK and beyond, and enables a range of online activities. He has written many articles on adult education and literature in English, including chapters in several books.

Hywel Dix taught English in India and Japan from 2003 until 2006. Subsequently, he was the Raymond Williams Research Fellow at the University of Glamorgan, which lead to the publication of *After Raymond Williams: Cultural Materialism and the Break-Up of Britain* (second edition, 2013). The approach of Hywel is significant for relocating his subject from the world of English literature to a European stage. Hywel is now Principal Academic in English and Communication at Bournemouth University where his writing on the 'break-up of Britain' has continued amid his wider interests in the relationship between literature, culture and political change in contemporary Britain.

Modern Wales by Parthian Books

The Modern Wales Series, edited by Dai Smith and supported by the Rhys Davies Trust, was launched in 2017. The Series offers an extensive list of biography, memoir, history and politics which reflect and analyse the development of Wales as a modernised society into contemporary times. It engages widely across places and people, encompasses imagery and the construction of iconography, dissects historiography and recounts plain stories, all in order to elucidate the kaleidoscopic pattern which has shaped and changed the complex culture and society of Wales and the Welsh.

The inaugural titles in the Series were *To Hear the Skylark's Song*, a haunting memoir of growing up in Aberfan by Huw Lewis, and Joe England's panoramic *Merthyr: The Crucible of Modern Wales*. The impressive list has continued with Angela John's *Rocking the Boat*, essays on Welsh women who pioneered the universal fight for equality and Daryl Leeworthy's landmark overview *Labour Country*, on the struggle through radical action and social democratic politics to ground Wales in the civics of common ownership. Myths and misapprehension, whether naïve or calculated, have been ruthlessly filleted in Martin Johnes' startling *Wales: England's Colony?* and a clutch of biographical studies will reintroduce us to the once seminal, now neglected, figures of Cyril Lakin, Minnie Pallister and Gwyn Thomas, whilst Meic Stehens' *Rhys Davies: A Writer's Life* and Dai *Smith's Raymond Williams: A Warrior's Tale* form part of an associated back catalogue from Parthian.

the RHYS DAVIES TRUST

WALES: ENGLAND'S COLONY?

Martin Johnes

From the very beginnings of Wales, its people have defined themselves against their large neighbour. This book tells the fascinating story of an uneasy and unequal relationship between two nations living side-by-side.

PB / £8.99
978-1-912681-41-9

RHYS DAVIES: A WRITER'S LIFE

Meic Stephens

Rhys Davies (1901-78) was among the most dedicated, prolific and accomplished of Welsh prose writers. This is his first full biography.

'This is a delightful book, which is itself a social history in its own right, and funny.'
– The Spectator

PB / £11.99
978-1-912109-96-8

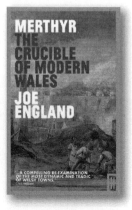

MERTHYR, THE CRUCIBLE OF MODERN WALES

Joe England

Merthyr Tydfil was the town where the future of a country was forged: a thriving, struggling surge of people, industry, democracy and ideas. This book assesses an epic history of Merthyr from 1760 to 1912 through the focus of a fresh and thoroughly convincing perspective.

PB / £18.99
978-1-913640-05-7

TO HEAR THE SKYLARK'S SONG

Huw Lewis

To Hear the Skylark's Song is a memoir about how Aberfan survived and eventually thrived after the terrible disaster of the 21st of October 1966.

'A thoughtful and passionate memoir, moving and respectful.'
– Tessa Hadley

PB / £8.99
978-1-912109-72-2

ROCKING THE BOAT

Angela V. John

This insightful and revealing collection of essays focuses on seven Welsh women who, in a range of imaginative ways, resisted the status quo in Wales, England and beyond during the nineteenth and twentieth centuries.

PB / £11.99
978-1-912681-44-0

TURNING THE TIDE

Angela V. John

This rich biography tells the remarkable tale of Margaret Haig Thomas (1883-1958) who became the second Viscountess Rhondda. She was a Welsh suffragette, held important posts during the First World War and survived the sinking of the *Lusitania*.

PB / £17.99
978-1-909844-72-8

BRENDA CHAMBERLAIN, ARTIST & WRITER

Jill Piercy

The first full-length biography of Brenda Chamberlain chronicles the life of an artist and writer whose work was strongly affected by the places she lived, most famously Bardsey Island and the Greek island of Hydra.

PB / £11.99
978-1-912681-06-8

PARTHIAN

MODERN WALES

RAYMOND WILLIAMS: A WARRIOR'S TALE

Dai Smith

Raymond Williams (1921-1998) was the most influential socialist writer and thinker in post-war Britain. Now, for the first time, making use of Williams' private and unpublished papers and by placing him in a wide social and cultural landscape, Dai Smith, in this highly original and much praised biography, uncovers how Williams' life to 1961 is an explanation of his immense intellectual achievement.

"Becomes at once the authoritative account... Smith has done all that we can ask the historian as biographer to do."
– Stefan Collini, *London Review of Books*

PB / £20
978-1-913640-08-8

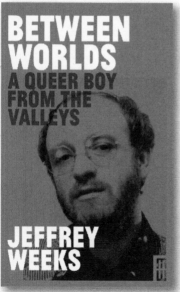

BETWEEN WORLDS: A QUEER BOY FROM THE VALLEYS

Jeffrey Weeks

A man's own story from the Rhondda. Jeffrey Weeks was born in the Rhondda in 1945, of mining stock. As he grew up he increasingly felt an outsider in the intensely community-minded valleys, a feeling intensified as he became aware of his gayness. Escape came through education. He left for London, to university, and to realise his sexuality. He has been described as the 'most significant British intellectual working on sexuality to emerge from the radical sexual movements of the 1970s'.

HB / £20
978-1-912681-88-4